The Journey to Finding You

Copyright © by Patrice Simmons, May 2016. All Rights Reserved.

First Printing, Asta Publications, LLC, trade paperback edition, May 2016

Scripture quotations, unless otherwise indicated, are taken from the New International Version (NIV) of the Bible.

No part of this publication may be produced or transmitted in any form or by any means without written permission of the author.

ISBN 13: 978-1-934947-97-5

Cover Designed by: Karina Tamayo

Printed in the United States of America

The Journey to Finding You

Patrice Simmons

Acknowledgements

I want to thank my Lord and savior for putting purpose in me, allowing me to birth it out for the world to see. My passion for writing is food to my soul; I'm blessed and thankful to God for His grace and mercy, and I continue to do His will for my life. No amount of fame or fortune will ever derail me from my purpose. When we connect ourselves to the Father, saying yes to His will and purpose for our lives, we open the door to the kingdom. God will continue to heed our requests for guidance, counsel, and love every day, and we will always be the people He created us to be.

I would like to acknowledge my mentor, Trent Shelton, a motivational speaker, author, and entrepreneur, as well as the creator and founder of Rehab Time. After watching countless videos containing his great messages about life, relationships, and God, I have been inspired to walk down my own path as a motivational speaker. I was inspired to create my weekly video series called, "Wednesday Wake-Up."

I want to thank my parents, Nate and Karen Massey. You both have been my number one supporters, encouragers, helpers, and teachers. You both have listened and provided your shoulders for me to lean on throughout my writing journey.

To my sister, Alisha, I thank you for teaching me about how to love yourself and for helping me to bring my vision to life. To my brother, Shawn, I thank you for your love, belief in me, and support of my writing.

To my friends and other family members, I thank you for your support and love. You are truly appreciated!

Introduction
Who Are You?

Life is a journey to be traveled through your own life experiences. You will not arrive at your destination until you go through the self-discovery process. Trials and personal circumstances are aligned for you to see the real meaning of life, and where you are going. It is most often difficult for us to achieve self-elevation. It is much easier to blame others for our shortcomings than it is to face our problems and the consequences of our choices! Along our journey we will be confronted with many situations, some filled with joy and laughter, some with heartaches. How we react to what we are faced with determines what the remainder of our journey will be like. Instead of ignoring our present situation and waiting on the future, we should focus on the experiences we're having right now.

There is never a moment during life when you will be any more alive than you are right now. Treating your hypothetical situation as more real than your current condition can demean the present moment. So focus on your goals and savor every part of your life. We should not act as though any part of life is something we are just getting through on the way to some destination. Throughout your adventure, people will give you advice and insights on how to live, but when it comes down to it, the only advice you should listen to is God's. He is the author and foundation of our lives. If you are not a believer, become one—it is the greatest relationship you will ever have. Live boldly and never stray from that!

Life is the way you view your journey, obstacles, and choices. You cannot make it in this world without seeking guidance and understanding from God. It doesn't matter if you are a doctor, lawyer, singer, dancer, etc. Nothing you do will ever amount to the knowledge and wisdom you gain from seeking God. "He is the way the truth and life. No one comes to the Father except through me." (John 14:6)

If you do not know where to turn for the understanding you desire, look for Him. He will bridge the gap of what you need to know so that you can live a successful and holy lifestyle. Only listen to people who are heading in the direction of greatness and who have the ability to help you get there. If you do not, you will have people all day telling you how to do this or that but not living in greatness themselves.

Know that our Heavenly Father is for us. Nothing can stand against us. Know that the devil is our enemy and that he is eternally defeated. Know who you are in Christ and walk in the reality of our new inheritance in creation.

Relationships are defined as the way in which two or more concepts, objects, or people are connected, or the way in which two or more people or organizations regard and behave toward one another.

Example: If you grew up experiencing pain and it was never treated correctly, it could become the focal point of your life. Your life experiences, however, teach you lessons and show you who you really are. I'm a firm believer that it is not what happens to you in life but how you handle yourself in challenging situations that makes the difference. Treat the problem as your solution, not as a true problem. This means you should not put energy into a problem except to focus on how you can turn it around and find a solution. Give yourself time to be upset about it, but do not let your feeling control you.

Relationships are one of the most valuable gifts you will ever experience in life. They are capable of brining you a great deal of joy, happiness, peace, understanding, and pleasure. The flipside of a positive relationship is a negative one, and oftentimes people experience the latter kind, which can involve pain, misery, unkind words, and lacking joy. The type of relationship you are in will determine the outcome of who you are going to be in life. It is very important that every connection you make in life is a positive, uplifting one. Never settle for anything negative, but count on God to deliver on his promises and bring beautiful people and connections into your life.

> "There is no better than adversity. Every defeat, every heartbreak, every loss, contains its own seed, its own lesson on how to improve your performance the next time." ~*Malcolm X*
>
> "If you want to become wealthy, work harder on yourself than at your job." ~*Jim Rohan*
>
> "Life is not a dress rehearsal, this is it!"
> ~*Mikki Taylor, Essence Magazine*
>
> "Make sure the outside of you is a good reflection of the inside of you." ~*Jim Rohn*
>
> "Opportunities and success are not something you go after necessarily but something you attract by becoming an attractive person." ~*Jim Rohn*

Life has a way of showing us just where we are now and how to get ourselves back on track if we have fallen off. For example, when you wake up in the morning, how do you feel? Are you thankful for another day? Are you happy to be alive or outright unhappy, wishing you had not awakened? I know this may seem a bit extreme, but it really is not. I have had mornings when I did not feel happy about my life nor did I want to wake up. These thoughts are directly connected to how you feel about the life you are living. When you think positively, hope for the best, and believe in brighter days, good things will happen for you. Thinking negatively does not help you grow as a person and things tend not to go well. It is vitally important for you to focus on the positive, as doing so will shape your world for the better. When I was unfocused, the challenges I faced got the better of me. With God on my side, I was delivered from my negative thoughts and was able to recognize my purpose and, ultimately, to make an impact in this world. Colossians 3:2 instructs us how to think correctly.

In every situation, regardless of the mitigating factors, you have the ability to change the way your mind reacts. If what you are thinking, saying, or doing in response to a particular circumstance or individual does not bring you peace, change your mindset! Changing your mind about something or someone transforms how that thing or person impacts your life. Certain paths you choose can change your life forever. Let us humble our hearts to our Almighty God.

"I will bring peace and mercy to my situation. I shall not walk in dark today for the Holy Spirit will guide me into all truth. The Lord will give me understanding in all things and wisdom and knowledge shall stabilize my times for I have the mind of Christ." (James 3:17; John 16:13)

God is love
God is the truth
God is the power

"You cannot judge the creation without judging the creator." ~*Iyanla Vanzant*

Set your mind, and keep it set, on what is above (the higher things) not on the things that are on the earth.

The Journey to Finding You will take you through a self-discovery process that will provide you with the opportunity to delve deep inside of yourself so you can identify the root of your problems and develop solutions to overcome them. It is through your increased faith and beliefs that you will recognize your purpose and experience a fulfilling life.

Table of Contents

Introduction..vii

Part I: Who Are You?

Chapter 1: How the Mind Works...................................1
Chapter 2: Environment..5
Chapter 3: Different Ranges of Classes........................10
Chapter 4: Beliefs..15
Chapter 5: Gender Roles: Male versus Females.............22
Chapter 6: Good Traits and Bad Traits.........................24
Chapter 7: Race..29
Chapter 8: Standards...32
Chapter 9: How We View Relationships......................34
Chapter 10: Character: What it Means to be in
    a Relationship...38
Chapter 11: Withdrawals/ No Deposits.......................41
Chapter 12: The Foundation is Love, God and Yourself....43

Part II: Where Are you Going in Life?

Chapter 13: History, Does that Make a Difference
    in a Relationship?..49
Chapter 14: Drama: Baby Mamas................................55
Chapter 15: The Greatest Gift of All is Love..................57
Chapter 16: Are You Pregnant?...................................59
Chapter 17: Is the Wait Worth It?................................61

Part III: Your Choices Chooses Your Destination

Chapter 18: Moving On..65
Chapter 19: Lust versus Love......................................68
Chapter 20: Single Life...72

Chapter 21: Married Life..76
Chapter 22: Obtaining and Maintaining...........................79
Chapter 23: Celebration..81
Chapter 24: Leadership...90
Chapter 25: You Choose..92
Chapter 26: The Cover Up...94

Part IV: A Deeper Look Within

Chapter 27: What If?...99
Chapter 28: Meditation Room.......................................103
Chapter 29: Heaven...106
Chapter 30: The Journey...110
Chapter 31: The Fundamentals of Life..........................112
Chapter 32: Patrice's Declaration Letter.......................114
Chapter 33: Purpose: What You Are Created For?........116
Chapter 34: Life Goals..119

Part V: Defining Your Purpose

Chapter 35: Destination..124
Chapter 36: Difficult Roads Often Lead to Beautiful
            Destinations..127
Chapter 37: Walk in Your Victory.................................129
Chapter 38: Kingdom..132
Chapter 39: Keys: What Do You Desire in Life?...........135
Chapter 40: Maya Angelou..138
Chapter 41: When I Think About Myself......................140

PART I:
WHO ARE YOU?

Chapter 1
How the Mind Works

We can take charge of our lives by taking charge of our minds.

Our mind is the capillary to the brain, which signals to us as we encounter different circumstances on a daily basis. Growing up, I enjoyed watching scary movies such as *Nightmare on Elm Street*, *Friday the 13th*, *Halloween*, and *Child's Play*. If you are a scary movie lover, like me, you understand the excitement I felt from watching, though some people think watching this type of movie is crazy. My mom did not understand why I liked movies that involved insane characters who killed people. Now let me make this very clear: I'm not crazy, nor do I enjoy watching people get hurt. Truthfully, I'm not sure why I like scary movies; it might be the thrill and the excitement that comes when watching the unexpected. But back to how the mind works. The mind works in three tiers: conscious, subconscious, and unconscious. They work together to create the reality in your life. And they can shape you into a happier, more peaceful, and confident person. This is the breakdown of all three parts of the mind.

Conscious mind: This level includes the feeling you get that something is not right about a person, place, and situation. The conscious mind can also be defined as intuition. Your conscious mind represents ten percent of your brain's capacity.

Subconscious: This level keeps track of your recent memories and is in continuous contact with the resources of your unconscious mind. For example, if you experienced a breakup or celebrated something important to you, your subconscious mind would keep track of it.

Unconscious: The unconscious mind consistently communicates with the other parts of the mind and provides us with the meaning to all our interactions with the world. The conscious mind acts as a filter that communicates to the outside world and the inner self through speech, pictures, writing, movement, thoughts, feelings, emotions, imagination, sensations, dreams, beliefs, and habits.

If you ever have strange or disturbing dreams, blame it on your unconscious mind. Watch your emotions and feelings, as they have a way of getting you in trouble at times. Choose to communicate wisely and make healthier decisions, so that your unconscious mind can play back positive thoughts, thus inspiring you to dream and enjoy your life.

Sigmund Freud, the founder of psychoanalysis, believed that people could be cured by making conscious their unconscious thoughts and motivations; his ideas provided a useful model for understanding the mind and how it works. A good analogy for describing how your conscious mind works is the keyboard and monitor. Data is input through the keyboard, and the results appear on the monitor screen. The subconscious mind is similar to the RAM in your computer. RAM, an acronym for random access memory, is a type of computer memory that is accessed randomly. RAM is used by the central processing unit (CPU) when a computer is running to store information that needs to be used very quickly, but it does not store any information permanently.

Your unconscious mind and subconscious mind act in a similar way, as you make sense of all the data you receive from the world to keep you safe and ensure your survival.

The way we structure our thoughts is how we view ourselves in the current state of the situation. A bad relationship, rocky marriage, loss of a job. They all contribute to how we view circumstances as well as the outcome of those circumstances. The goal is to focus the mind on only the positive, even if it seems difficult. Train your mind to believe and see the greater good. Trust the process that God is allowing you to go through.

Joyce Meyers puts it this way in her book, *The Mind Connection: How the Thoughts You Choose Affect Your Mood, Behavior, and Decisions*: thoughts can seem random and meaningless are actually connected to your well-being and impact your life every day. What you think affects your words, attitudes, decisions, and emotions. Your thoughts influence how you relate to yourself, to other people, and to God. The good news is that God has equipped you to take control of your thinking and increase your happiness.

Our thoughts control our actions and behavior.

It is important for you to make the right decisions when you are faced with challenging situations. And if you miss the mark, forgive yourself and start a new day. Do not allow outside forces to control you any longer. With God's help you can begin thinking positively, which will cause you to change the direction of your life.

Bible verses to inspire you:

A right mind (Mark 5:15)
A humble mind (Philippians2:3)
A transformed mind (Romans 12:2)
A spiritual mind (2 Corinthians 7:7)
A ready mind (2 Corinthians 8:19)
A renewed mind (Ephesians 4:23)
And do not be conformed to this world, but be transformed by the renewing of your mind, that you may prove what is good and acceptable and perfect will of god. (Romans12:2)

I can safely say that if you need a change in any area of your life, it will start with changing your mindset.

Change your world through positive thinking and living.

Five tips for maintaining a positive mind:

1. Seek wisdom from God daily.
2. Believe in yourself to change the thought pattern in your life.
3. Meditate on the word of God daily.
4. When a negative thought starts to sink in, remind yourself why a positive one has to stay.
5. Be determined to control your mind.

As soon as I started to control my thoughts and focus on positive ones, I began to believe in the greater good of my situation, even when it seemed as though I had no way out. My world changed for the better.

I believe in you. Changing your thoughts will change your life.

Chapter 2
Environment

The surroundings or conditions in which a person, animal, or plant lives or operates.

When you think about environment, what comes to mind? Spaces, community, earth, health, and how things work? Well, our environment has everything to do with the outcome of our relationships. Let me explain.

I grew up in Baltimore, Maryland, in the early 1980s. The '80s seemed much better in ways than the current times. As children we were able to freely play outside and walk to school by ourselves without worrying about being kidnapped. Music had meaning and even helped mold me as a person. Now do not get me wrong: today's music today is not all bad; it just is not the same anymore. Back then, people looked out for each other more; family, teachers, and the church community were all involved in our development. It seemed as though in the '80s children demonstrated a lot more respect for their elders and authority figures. During those times, it appeared as if there were not many single-parent homes, and parents were more attuned with their children. Women were treated with more respect by men during that time as well. Queen Latifah's song "Unity," released in November 1993, depicts the misogynistic way women were treated in society. She took a stand for women's rights and addressed the issues faced by women.

So what changed? Today's environment teaches us that it is okay for women to call one another "bitches" and "hoes," even being called a "thot" is accepted. "Thot" is a new term for me. Phrases such as "that hoe over there" are used to refer to women. *Really? How nice does that sound?* Additionally, women fight each other to gain respect. We no longer show reverence toward each other as women. Twenty-one years later, this is how we view and treat each other. We have to learn to demonstrate respect, love, care, and concern for each other. We must be our brothers' and sisters' keepers. It truly saddens my heart to view videos of recorded fights on the Internet, which encourages negative behavior. *What happened to caring for one another, sticking together, and bonding with each other? Have those days really faded away to the point that now everyone is out for themselves only, showing no heart or compassion?*

I implore you not to take a back seat and continue watching this negative behavior in our communities. Be proactive and create positivity around you. Whether it is reconstructing a playground, visiting an elderly home, or clearing trash. Help a neighbor with groceries or shovel snow in their driveway. Set morals, principles, and values, so that our environment and our communities become better, as they were in the '80s. Darren Hardy from Success Magazine described success in this way: "The secret to a truly successful life is doing more of what you love and less of what you do not. Regularly remind yourself of your personal version of success. Share your success, whether or not they fit society's definition."

Nothing can be more disheartening than seeing your community and environment crumble or go to wayside, as if no one cares. In my opinion, my hometown of Baltimore has really gone downhill over the last few years. I remember when I was ten years old I had to walk to school, which was located twenty minutes from my house. I had no issues going there or coming home safely. The children in the community felt safe, as it was part of our normal routine.

My mom would take me shopping on Green Mount and 33rd Street, which used to be called "the Stripe." The Stripe is where most of us bought our clothing. I used to love that area, as it was well maintained. The community cared and I loved going there. Fast-forward twenty years and I would not dare walk to school alone, go to the grocery store, or go near Green Mount. *Why*? I have seen the community change drastically, and it is no longer safe.

People no longer appear to care about what happens in their community. It is like they see the pain and despair but have chosen not to take action. Although I no longer live in Baltimore, the church I am involved in provides outreach services to the community. I am committed to the city I grew up in and believe that one of my purposes in life is to make it a safe place again. If you live in an environment or community that has changed for the worse, do what you can to take that community back.

Tips on how you can take your community back:

- Stop with the lazy talk and take action!
- Get involved in many outreach programs that will help your community to be a better place.
- Show true acts of kindness, love, and care.
- Keep God as the focus, never separate yourself from Him.
- Love and give more

My Prayer

Lord, this earth belongs to you and your purpose creating it has been fulfilled. We run around and destroy your trees, crops, and animals for our own satisfaction. You created us in your image to be beautiful, wonderful, loving, and kind people. But we have not been loving or kind. Instead we are running around in this world killing one another, raping our young girls and boys, sexually assaulting our elderly women, and disrespecting our teachers, who are there to educate us. We are blinded by our selfish acts and behavior and use social media as a platform to gain popularity and acceptance, when the only acceptance we need is from you. We scroll down our Facebook timelines looking for the latest gossip, and the news broadcasts drama and issues. Liking and sharing negative posts, we ignore the positives ones. We have made social media our daily priority instead of seeking you, the King of Kings, our God for guidance and understanding. We spend money on material things—cars, clothing, etc.—while homeless people walk around needing our help; we give them looks of disdain when they ask for money. We spend our time watching television, participating in hobbies, and otherwise being unproductive, all while allowing our communities to continue to struggle.

We have the time to record fights of women, young girls, and boys, as they destroy themselves. We watch these videos as though they were our personal entertainment. We have lost sight of who we are and what we have been created to be. I'm sorry for allowing myself to become sidetracked by the ills of this world. I will do my share to help build this place you created for me live in. I help young children to be the best they can be and remain an example for them. I will strive each day to be a women of God, a person who has integrity, a good heart, love and genuine care for others. I will live my purpose and help other people with theirs. I will continue to exhibit excellence when building your kingdom. I will represent you in my daily life and actions. I will live to serve you and chase after you, oh Lord. I love you and honor your holy name. Amen.

Chapter 3
Different Ranges of Classes

In America, the working class is considered synonymous with low class. The working class has been categorized as having a lower socioeconomic status due to low income, lack of skills and education, and work in mostly manual jobs. Oftentimes, those classified as having low socioeconomic status are overlooked and misjudged by their behavior and social status.

When you think of lower class, what comes to your mind? A single woman on welfare with a lot of children by multiple fathers? Someone without a job or car, loud-mouthed, no morals or goals, low self-esteem, rude, ghetto? These people are also often viewed as being drug abusers, ex-convicts, or prostitutes. These people just exist in the world versus creating opportunities for themselves to live a better life. *Do you see where am going with this?* All of these things I mentioned are nothing more than stereotypes and judgement. People who are from a lower socioeconomic class do not necessarily fit the stereotypes; their circumstances and or status does not define them. Those who conduct themselves in ways that are unbecoming still deserve to be treated with respect and dignity, regardless of their status. It is important that we look beyond people's conduct and love them in a manner that will not make them feel as though they are less than human.

I remember watching the movie, *The Blind Side* starring Sandra Bullock. The movie is based on the true story of Leigh

Anne and Sean Tuohy, a well-to-do white family who take in a homeless Mike "Big Mike" Oher, an African American teenager, and help him fulfill his potential. The Tuohy family looked beyond his socioeconomic status and loved him the way God loves us.

Many of us have experienced times when we have struggled financially. We might have had to apply for food stamps, the special supplemental nutrition known as Women, Infants, and Children (WIC), or Medicaid, and we might have shopped at thrift stores, etc. *Does this mean that we should be looked down on or treated as though we are less than human?* Absolutely not; it simply means that we need assistance to help us through a challenging time. No one is lower class, even though society has created different systems to identify who we are. We have to love all people the same—the trash man, McDonald's employee, and the janitor are all people who deserve to be treated with kindness and respect.

Remember to always do the following:

- Love
- Respect
- Be kind

Another socioeconomic group, the middle class, includes professionals, business workers, and their families. A stereotypical middle-class family might consist of a two-parent family living in a detached home with a well-maintained garden. Their children go to college, they have dinner parties, they drink wine, many cookbooks can be found in the home, and Dad is home by 6 p.m. to help the children with their homework. In my opinion, the middle-class community has a comfortable standard of living, significant income, financial security, and considerable work autonomy, relying on their expertise to sustain themselves. I would consider my family to be part of the middle class. My mother is an entrepreneur and owned a hair salon and currently owns a modeling agency. We were not on public assistance nor did we live in public housing. We lived in a big house, had our own bedrooms, attended good schools, and shopped weekly. After I graduated from the fifth grade, my parents relocated my siblings and me to what we call the country. What a difference scenery can make. We did not have the best of everything, but my parents ensured that we did not go without.

My dad worked two jobs and bought me my first car when I was fourteen years old. Growing up, I really felt privileged to have hard-working parents who provided our family with the best life possible.

As a business woman and assistant manager who lives in a nice community located in the country with a nice car, I'm considered middle class as well. Financially my family is doing well and my goal is to become a full-time entrepreneur. Even though I am considered middle class, I do not look down on others; instead, I help build people up, encouraging them to strive for more and realize their greatest potential. It is important that we teach, support, and motivate others to achieve greatness.

Remember to do the following:

- Reach
- Believe
- Seek to help other to achieve their greatness

The upper class is considered to be the wealthiest layer in American society and is often referred to as the rich, the aristocrats, and people born with silver spoons. Individuals of this class tend to be influential in politics, economic institutions, and public opinion. People from this class are composed of members born into this class or old money as well as those who have acquired wealth and influence within their own generation—the nouveau riche—such as celebrities. When you see celebrities with their fast cars, huge homes, flashy jewelry, and expensive trips, you dream of having these things too. This class is defined strictly in terms of wealth, possessions, and material things. Do not get me wrong: upper-class people in my opinion tend to be hardworking, focused, and driven. I think individuals from this social class do not allow challenges or obstacles deter them from reaching their goals or disrupting their lifestyle. They are motivated go-getters, unstoppable forces that never quit.

I admire the upper class and I am on the road of becoming one. I truly believe and feel that one of the ways of increasing my social class is having will power. I believe that God created us to be all that we can be, and the choice and will to fulfill our potential lies within each of us, regardless of our social class. I believe that we can all experience personal greatness if we strive for it. Everybody wants the reward, but oftentimes we do not want to work hard to do what it takes to achieve it. Many upper-class individuals work hard in their careers, travel to events, and read books to further themselves along. As I mentioned before we are all in this together and no one is better than the next. What really separates us is the level of hard work we choose to put into our daily lives. Achieving everything you're capable of requires changing your focus and changing your mindset. If you do not know your purpose, find your passion—it will be your guide into finding your purpose.

Tips:

- Pray and ask God to open your heart and mind to what the world needs from you.
- Seek Godly counsel from successful people who will help you throughout your journey.
- Say yes, even when you want to say no to hard work. It will pay off with great rewards.
- Be a leader. Follow no one's path but your own!
- Fail at it, but never give up.
- Have faith and trust God's process
- Be a lifelong learner!

Chapter 4
Beliefs
When Life is Great, Pray

Every behavior is motivated by a belief. The greatest gift in life is your belief, which is defined as accepting that a statement is true or that something exists. With that said, we must trust, have faith, and have confidence in someone or something. *Doesn't that sound great?* Believing in something higher than you is considered belief. Now that I have defined what belief means, I would like to pose a question to you: *What if you lived in a world where there was nothing to believe in? How would you live and view the world as a whole? Would morals, values, principles, integrity, and knowing right from wrong matter as much? How would you look at yourself?* I know this is a great deal to ponder, but it emphasizes how important belief is to life. It will shape the core of who you are, the way you view life. Once you come to terms with who you are, you will no longer get involved with bad relationship, and bad habits will no longer have power over you. This will only happen for you if you allow your belief in a higher provide guidance over your life.

Let me take this a step further for you. I remember being at work one day and a co-worker gave me a book that completely changed my outlook on life. No it was not the Bible, although the Bible has shaped and molded who I am today. The book was called *The Purpose Driven Life* by Rick Warren. What a powerful book! One of the things I truly loved was how Warren spoke about God and how to live our lives through Christ. One chapter in particular spoke to me: "Day 22 Created to Become Like Christ."

A brief summary of the chapter can be found below:

You were created to become like Christ. From the very beginning, God's plan has been to make you like his son, Jesus. Being like Christ is all about transforming your character, not your personality. Wow, right? Life is truly about what you believe and living in accordance with those beliefs. If you are a Christian, as I am, then your belief is in Jesus Christ. Knowing that he died for our sins and rose from the dead, and that the Bible contains instructions on how to live, is very inspiring and comforting. We must obey God's commands to have a fulfilled life. Muslims believe that the message of Allah, the creator, was given to several prophets, including Muhammad, Noah, Abraham, Moses, Elijah, and Jesus. Jehovah's Witnesses believe God is the Creator and Supreme Being, separate from the Son, Jesus Christ, and they reject the trinity doctrine.

It does not matter what you believe in, as there are several religious beliefs. What is most important is that you believe in something other than yourself. Having a belief system helps to develop and mold you into a purposeful human being. There is no point in going through life not believing or discovering that there is more to life then what you can see. Knowing that God has created earth for us is more than enough for us and affords us the ability to live our best lives. Before concluding this chapter, I'm going to share a story with you that I pray will open your eyes to how important it is to believe in God.

I once dated a guy for about five months; he was six years younger than me and did not have children, while I have four children. He was a very nice guy I had met at a networking event. We began talking after he overheard a conversation

I was having with another person about religion. Having faith and believing in God are high on my list of qualities I want for a man in my life, and he certainly made the cut. After about a few weeks the man I thought believed in the same thing I did turned out to be my worst nightmare. He was a "Hebrew Israelite," and they only believe in the Old Testament and customs. They do not believe in Jesus nor that he died for our sins. He also believed in polygamy. He told me that I was going to be his unlawful wife, move to Africa with him, and convert my beliefs to the Israel way.

I did not know of these beliefs at first because he waited until he was comfortable with me to share them. Being the strong-minded Christian woman I am, I ended the relationship. I knew that this would not work out with how different our beliefs were. The lesson I learned was to remain strong and steadfast in my faith and belief in God. When you know who you are, no one can derail you from your beliefs.

Always remain true to yourself and your beliefs. Never let go of that, because there will be people who will test your faith, morals, and values. Please uphold your integrity and character, as doing so will take you a long way in life. God is the foundation of my life and holds the keys to my heart. I live my life according to God's standards, and it is because of this relationship that I was able to let go of that relationship before it was too late.

Encourage people to always believe that something other than themselves exists in this world. Hold true to your belief and be that light and example for others. This is our greatest privilege, our immediate destiny.

Prayer is one of the greatest ways to connect with God. When praying, it is important that you are specific about your needs. The promises of God are so great to those who truly pray. He puts Himself fully into the hands of those who pray. Come to him with a pure heart, believing with all you have, and he will deliver to you in his time, according to his plan for your life. Trust in his word and you will never lose faith. If your situation does not look like it is going to change for the better, look to the Lord, and trust that he will give you the strength, courage, and wisdom to prevail.

My Prayer

Oh Lord, search my heart and strip it from the darkness that I allow to reside inside me. Remove any malice, bitterness, and judgment that I have toward anyone, so that I can strive for forgiveness. Help me to seek your truth daily and correct me when I'm wrong. For I know you are the only way I can get into the Kingdom to be with you.

Bible Verses:

"All things are possible to him who believes." (Mark 9:23)

"Ask, and it will be given to you seek, and you will find, knock, and it will be opened to you." (Matthew 7:7)

"Therefore I tell you, whatever you ask in prayer, believe that you have received it, and it will be yours." (Mark 11:24)

"Do not be anxious about anything, but in every situation, by prayer and petition, with thanksgiving, present you requests to God. And the peace of God, which transcends all understanding, will guard your hearts and your minds in Christ Jesus." (Philippians 4:6-7)

"Let us then approach God's throne of grace with confidence, so that we may receive mercy and find grace to help us in our time of need." (Hebrews 4:16)

"But when you pray, go into your room, close the door and pray to your father, who is unseen. Then your father, who sees what is done in secret, will reward you." (Matthew 6:6)

"But to you who are listening I say: Love your enemies, do

good to those who hate you, bless those who curse you, pray for those who mistreat you." (Luke 6:27-28)

The Serenity Prayer

God grant me the serenity;
To accept the things I cannot change;
Courage to change the things I can;
And wisdom to know the difference.
Living one day at a time; enjoying one moment at a time;
Accepting hardships as the pathway to peace;
Taking, as He did, this sinful world as it is, not as I would have it;
Trusting that he will make all things right if I surrender to His will;
So that I may be reasonably happy in this life
And supremely happy with Him forever and ever in the next.
Amen.

Chapter 5
Gender Roles (Males versus. Female)

Gender roles are cultural and personal. They determine how males and females should think, speak, and model ourselves according to his image. A man is to lead his family and take charge in the world, be strong, and carry his weight in life. God teaches us to respect and honor the gender roles that we have been placed in, as these roles help us to deal with one another.

Men are from Mars and Women are from Venus is a true statement. Sometimes it seems as though men are out of touch with us women and that we are really two different creatures existing in the same universe. We think differently and respond to things differently. In my opinion, men were raised to be emotionless, strong, and heads of their households. Manhood begins at an early age, before men reach adulthood, and in some cases before they are equipped with the tools needed to survive. In contrast, women are raised to rely on their instincts to make decisions and navigate in this world. It is my view that women are maternal, can be emotional, and tend to mature faster. At a young age, girls are taught to be independent and learn how to cook and clean.
It is my belief that women are more prepared for this world than men. My statements and beliefs do not refer to all men and women. Scripture (Genesis 1:27) states that God created them, male and female. Even though the statement Men are from Venus applies to certain situations, God's word says that we truly are all the same, shaped and molded in his likeness.

Women, I want to leave you with this:

We are wonderfully and beautifully made from God, we have the tenderness of a mother's love, and we help to groom our men. Our strength and courage is undeniable, especially when we are faced with adversity. We move past negativity because we know that it will not help us to get to the next level. We are wives, mothers, teachers, dreamers, and believers. We are the backbone of our families. Speak these words daily, believe in yourself, and always love the women God created you to be.

Remember to be:

- Honest
- Gentle
- Humble
- Loving, caring, brave
- We are one, we are united, and we are each other keeper!

To my men:

You are the leaders of our community and homes. The fathers to our daughters and sons, as you are the role models who show them how to be the best they can be. Show your sons the right path to take and never allow them to feel inadequate. Raise them to be God-fearing men, good husband and fathers, and leaders in their communities.

Chapter 6
Good and Bad Traits

Love, joy, peace, patience, kindness, goodness, faithfulness, gentleness, and self-control are all positive traits one should desire to have.

"Character is like a tree and reputation like a shadow. The shadow is what we think of it; the tree is the real thing."
~Abraham Lincoln

God looks at the attitude of your heart.

How do you respond to negative people? You should respond to them with compassion, empathy, honesty, faith, peace and joy. The ability to be open-minded and intellectual, and to have a thirst for knowledge is an ongoing process. Good work ethics and eagerness to assist and learn will help you to progress in life. Other characteristics that will help you reach your goals include having the ability to control anger in a healthy manner, knowing how to converse, knowing your limits and meeting your expectations, having high self-esteem, knowing yourself and loving yourself so that you are able to love others.

When you have bad traits, they shape the way you see the world. How you handle shortcomings will be based on those bad traits.

Here are a few bad traits—*do you see yourself in any one of them?*

- Messiness
- Selfishness
- Ego
- Prideful
- Arrogance, as we all know is bad but having self-confidence is a good trait just be careful with how you act.
- Shyness
- Distracted
- Neuroticism- A person who respond with negative emotions to threat, frustration, or loss.
- Laziness

According to LiveBoldAndBloom.com, good character consists of defining your values and integrity based on the time-tested principles of self-reflection and courage.

Ten Ways to Improve Your Character:

1. Integrity: Integrity is having strong morals, principles, and core values. As a person with integrity, you conduct your life based on those main beliefs as your guide. When you have integrity, you adhere to those values, whether or not people are watching.
2. Honesty: Honesty is more than telling the truth; it is living the truth. It is being straightforward and trustworthy in all of your interactions, relationships, and thoughts. Being honest requires self-honesty and authenticity.
3. Loyalty: Loyalty is faithfulness and devotion to your loved ones, your friends, and anyone with whom you have a trusted relationship. Loyalty can also extend to your employer, the organizations you belong to, your community,

and your country.
4. Respectfulness: You treat yourself and others with courtesy, kindness, deference, dignity, and civility. You offer basic respect as a sign of your values toward all people.

    You see the worth in all people and you are able to accept their inherent flaws.
5. Humility: You have a confident yet modest opinion of your own self-importance. You do not see yourself as "too good" for other people or situations. Your mindset favors learning and growth, and you have the desire to express and experience gratitude for what you have rather than expecting that you deserve more.
6. Generosity: You are willing to offer your time, energy, efforts, emotions, words, or assets without the expectation of something in return. You offer these freely and often joyously.
7. Compassion: You feel deep sympathy and pity for those who are suffering and experiencing misfortune, and you have desire to alleviate their suffering.
8. Forgiveness: You make conscious, intentional decisions to let go of resentment and anger toward someone for an offense—whether or not forgiveness is sought by the offender. Forgiveness may or may not include pardoning, restoration, or reconciliation. It extends both to others and to one's self.
9. Lovingness: The ability to be loving toward those you love means showing them through your words, actions, and expressions how deeply you care about them. It includes the willingness to be open and vulnerable.
10. Conscientiousness: You have the desire to do things well or to the best of your ability. You are thorough, careful, efficient, organized, and vigilant in your efforts, based on your own principles or sense of what is right.

Good character can include the following attributes:

- Attracts the trust and respect of other people
- Allows you to influence others
- Changes your perspective about failure
- Sustains you through difficult times or opposition
- Improves your self-esteem, self-respect, and confidence
- Creates a foundation for happy and healthy relationships
- Helps you stay committed to your values and goals
- Improves your chances of success in work and in other endeavors
- Shows you your own worthiness
- Helps you regain confidence, belief, and hope
- Helps you believe anything is possible
- Encourages willingness to help others
- Drives people to strive for greatness in life
- Encourages you to seek wisdom
- Negate from negativity

The bottom line is that you should strive to have good traits. Be the best you possible and maintain positive thinking. Be motivated and eager to help others in times of need. Your efforts to being a kind, understanding, and loving person will be favored by God.

When people try to tell me who I'm not, I have to remind them that the God I serve thinks the world of me and that his opinion of who I am is the only opinion I care about. I encourage you to do the same. *Why?* Sometimes people try to make you think you are not good enough or worthy to have great things in this world. Instead of supporting and believing in you, these people will make you feel miserable, as they are. Know that you are somebody in Jesus. He is the author and finisher of your faith. Put your all into to Him, not man. God will never leave you nor forsake you.

Chapter 7
Race

We are not here on earth to see through each other; we are here to see each other through.

Black
Caucasian
Asian
Native American or Pacific Islander

When you think about these different races what comes to mind? Most Black people's ancestors were enslaved. Slavery is an important part of history and has impacted the world. Even though this is the 21st century, racism still exists even if some of us believe it does not. *Why?* Racism has been a part of human history since the beginning of time. Racism is defined as a belief that race is the primary determinant of human traits and capacities and that those racial differences produce an inherent superiority of a particular race. Our society and its forbearers have successfully managed to plant the seeds of discrimination into our consciousness long before we were able to assert our choices.

Slavery and serfdom have been identified as the blackest spots on the face of human civilization. History has provided us with insight into our glorious and shameful past. Historical acts serve as lessons to guide us and ultimately determine our future course of action. History will repeat itself if we do not learn from our mistakes as a society. Racism still exists today, in the 21st century. Discrimination and injustices against people of color can be seen in the workplace, legal system, and in communities, to name a few. Our communities are suffering as a result of guns, drugs, liquor stores on every corner, and menacing police officers can be seen appearing to be waiting for the opportunity to target our people. It seems that White communities are not riddled with liquor stores on every corner, there are fewer drugs and limited police presence.

So who is to blame for this? We are to blame for all of this going on. We have first to remember everything in life is based on our choices and how we handle those decisions will ultimately result in a positive or negative outcome. Unfortunately, slavery did happen and had put Black people in a disparate position, but it is time to stop using that as a crutch or an excuse to not better ourselves.

Generation after generation has to give us the opportunity to impact our communities in a constructive way. We are the change that needs to happen, not Whites or any other race or ethnicity. All groups of people suffer from something negative in their communities, but as a Black person, I want to see a progressive change in my community. No more judging others based off of race, ethnicity, religion, creed, etc.; it is time for Black people to stop feeling as if they are not good enough, or that White people are the enemy. As a country, we must learn to lean on God for direction, trust His ways, and follow His guidance so that our America can be the way God designed it to be a long time ago.

As a country, we should resonate with Dr. Martin Luther King Jr.'s "I Have a Dream," speech and respect those who became before us and worked hard for our civil rights. We must remember that we are Americans. Above all, love each other deeply because love covers over a multitude of sins. Offer hospitality to one another without grumbling or complaining.

Chapter 8
Standards

The quality of a leader is reflected in the standards they set for themselves.

Standard is defined as a level of quality, achievement, etc., that is considered acceptable or desirable. Additionally, the standard is something that is excellent, and that is used to make judgments about the quality of other things.

When you start something such as a new career, school, relationship, organization, and or association, it assumed that there will be standards in place for you abide. I believe that the level of standards you set for yourself should inform people how to treat you. Never be a part of something that will cause you to lower your standards or make you feel bad for having them, as it will take away the quality of your life. For example, let say you start thinking about a new career path and it requires you to go to school to obtain a degree or certificate. I suggest that you consider the following:

Is this something am passionate about?
Does it represent the best of who I am?
Will it increase my level of excellence?
Will it shape me into being a better person?

Keep in mind that there is a difference between having a job versus a career. A job is where you get a paycheck to pay bills, buy clothing, and other essentials. Whereas, a career is a journey that includes all of your jobs, experiences, education, and training in the same field and requires lots of sacrifice, commitment, drive, hard work, and dedication. For example, a prospectively registered nurse has three educational paths to consider such as a: Associate degree in Nursing or Bachelor of Science degree in Nursing, take and pass the Nursing Council Licensure Examination, and apply for your state licensure. Being a registered nurse demonstrates to others that you have standards, a level of competence, and dedication to the field.

When you have your standards, it shows your level of love for God and how He wants you to do things in excellence. Let your name add value to who you are. God wants us to live our life according to His plan, the right way. Having standards shows that you have invested in yourself, and that is the best part of being a human being. When you start investing in you, you will notice that everything else will fall into place. Nothing shapes your life more than the standards that you set and the level of commitment you choose to make. When the right standards are put into your life, it will enhance your goals, dreams, and desires.

Never lower your standards for anyone or anything, teach people to meet you at your level of excellence. Self-respect is everything, knowing yourself is everything; they are the keys to unlocking the best part of you. Most importantly, never apologize for having high standards, the right people will appreciate that and rise to meet your expectations. Remember, having standards demonstrates your respect and that you have set the bar high for God. Keep striving for greatness and He will reward you.

Chapter 9
How We View Relationships

Rick Warren speaks about broken fellowship in his book. "The Purpose Driven Life," which a great segue into this chapter about relationships. A brief summary is found below: "Relationships are always worth restoring because life is all about learning how to love. God wants us to value relationships and make the effort to maintain them instead of discarding them whenever there is a rift or conflict. God has given us the ministry of restoring and building a relationship. Christ wants His family to be known for the love we have for each other. Broken fellowship and relationships are considered to be a disgraceful testimony to unbelievers."

Thanks, Pastor Warren for your words on this subject.

God has restored our relationship with Him through Christ and has given us this ministry of restoring relationships.
(2 Corinthians 5:18)
God wants us to grow up like Christ in everything.
(Ephesians 4:15)
We are not meant to remain as children. (Ephesians 4:14)

Recently, I began thinking about the way us, as humans, view relationships. In the average human mind, being in a relationship and being in love is seen as the ultimate happiness, the highest goal to achieve and accomplishment possible. I know this to be true because my greatest desire is love and have a relationship with a God fearing man. Nothing drives me more than watching romantic movie and or show. Every time, I see a romantic film, I am reminded of the love I seek and just how badly I need someone in my life.

Now, I do not see anything wrong with having a love desire or longing to have a person. But what I discovered was that the way I dealt with that longing was obsessive. God has a way of showing and providing you with your needs. If you do not follow His instructions you can self-destruct. I had to remind myself that my love for God should be my ultimate desire and achievement. God is love, and He represents that in everything.

I have had several conversations with family friends about the topic of relationships. There were varying views on the subject. Some people felt that a relationship of any sort taught you about life and yourself. Others felt that a relationship is an investment; what you put into is what you will get in return. That view resonated with me and reminded of my pastor's words, 'some people accept a harvest with no seeds or deeds planted. People will make a lot of withdrawals in your life, without depositing anything back. If you find yourself being in a particular friendship or relationship that just seems to be stuck in a rut, that is not healthy, and it will bring in a lot of negativity and unnecessary drama.

According to Mattingly, Lewandowski, and McIntyre, our relationships can change our self- concepts in two ways. First, the size of your self-concept can change. You can develop new traits, or your existing one can be more prominent. For example, a man dates someone that prepares elaborate meals, and he has discovered a passion for gourmet cuisine. If that person stops making those types of meals, his expectation of receiving gourmet meal has been lost. Do not neglect yourself. You can learn to cook gourmet yourself. Another example is of a woman who may no longer feel that her husband finds her attractive. She believes that her husband's thoughts and opinions about her appearance define her. Secondly, your self-concept could change--that is, the extent to which you perceive these changes about yourself as being positive or negative. In some cases, a negative relationship could bring about positive self-concept changes, personal strengths as it forces you to deal with the complexities of the relationship. The size and outlook about of our self-concept can shift. There are four distinct types of self-concept changes that can occur as our relationships progress and becomes interdependent.

Four Distinct Types of Self-Concept:

1. *Self-expansion*: We add new, positive, information to the self-concept. This can happen as we incorporate aspects of our partner's personalities into our own and engage in stimulating activities with our partners.
2. *Self-contraction*: We lose positive self-concept content. Example, a man may be an avid baseball fan, but when his wife refuses to watch games with him, his interest wanes.
3. *Self-pruning*: We lose or suppress negative self-concept content. Self- pruning improves the self-concept. Those who are married are not as lonely as single people. Our partners can help us purge undesirable traits such as smoking, weight gain, etc.
4. *Self-adulteration*: We gain negative traits, this can occur when being in the relationship consistently changes your behavior for the worse. Having verbal disagreements that involve yelling and harsh words towards one another will over time turn you into a critical person.

For me, a sufficient relationship to have is one with God. It is the start of a healthy path and will show you every aspect of what you want, do not want, need and do not need, how to be how and how not to be. Every human being needs this type of shaping and molding in their lives. You can develop this strength and level of confidence with God's help. He will change how you view relationships.

Chapter 10
Character: What it Means to be in a Relationship

It is a character that makes you a person of quality. Your looks will attract a person, but your character will keep them.

A character is defined as the mental and moral qualities distinctive to an individual. Character traits are all the aspects of a person's behavior and attitudes that make up that person. You meet an amazingly gorgeous man who looks like Denzel Washington, and his eyes and lips are like Idris Elba. You have a great conversation over the phone, as you talked for hours. Now it is time to schedule your first date. You make plans to meet up on Saturday afternoon. He asked you where you like to hang out. He picks you up around 4:00 pm, you open the door and in front of you is this stunning, tall man, smelling like a million bucks standing in front of you. In your mind, you are saying, *"Lord where has he been all my life?"* He greets you with a nice smile and hands you a bouquet of roses before you head out for your date. While at your favorite restaurant he compliments you on how great you look; the night is going great with good conversation, good food, and everything looks picture perfect. You end the night not too late, and he kisses you on the cheek before leaving. He calls you the next day for another date, and you oblige. You go on another date, and it is just as perfect as the first one, and you inquire about seeing each other exclusively. He agrees, to it, and tells you how much he appreciates you and how amazing he thinks you are. A few weeks go by, and you begin to see the real him. His character traits that were hidden from you suddenly appear out of nowhere. You notice that his calls and text messages have lessened and are mostly late in the evening. You are no longer going on dates. It appeared that he only wanted to spend time having sex with you. You did not want to have sex with him so early, but you trusted him and convinced yourself that it was okay. You sent him a friend request on Facebook, but he never accepts. You begin to question what is wrong with this guy, why is acting so differently. Then you decided to investigate who this man is by checking his Facebook page since it was public and you discovered that he is married with five children. As you look through his family pictures, shock waves go through you. You also found out that he was bi-sexual and was intimate with another man when you glanced at an email that was sent to his phone. Disbelief sets in, and you wonder how he could do this to you. He seemed so perfect, yet he was far from it. He was the one in your mind.

Here is the problem most times when you meet someone new; you get to encounter their agent first. Through the course of time is when the real person reveals. You see character is what remains with you, looks do not. We have to learn the differences between nature and outside appearances. It is important that you discover a person's bad traits, and make your decision based off of the individual's character. Look deep within yourself before giving yourself to someone. Ask God to show and tell you the purpose the person will have in your life. Your character will always keep you grounded in all the great qualities of a person.

For this very reason, make every effort to add to your faith goodness; and to goodness, knowledge; and to knowledge, self-control; and to self-control, perseverance; and to perseverance, godliness; and to godliness, mutual affection; and to mutual affection, love. (2 Peter 1:5-7)

Chapter 11
Withdrawals/No Deposits

Do you know someone that only calls you when they want something? Or do you know someone that only reaches out to you when they need money or help?

Do you have or had a friend who seemed to take more of the relationship than they gave? If your response is yes, those types of people are called users and needy. If your response is no, you can call yourself lucky. These people seem to suck the life right out of you, and you feel drained every time you are around them. I do not believe that the majority of these people do not see themselves as users and do not want to treat people that way. It is my belief that these individuals have not developed the skills necessary to be independent and in some cases their value system is off. They only see things their way. Every situation is different, and it is up to you to determine whether or not these people add value and positivity to your life or not. If they are negative, and only take from you, then it is time to part ways. No one deserves nor needs a person who is going to make a lot of withdrawals from you without depositing something back into your life. Relationships are about given and take. What you put into it, is what you get in return. Needy people have developed a skill of being self-absorbed, and when they cannot get what they want from you, they tend to play the victim and do not see their behavior as improper. I used to have a friend who was needy and selfish. She only did things for her benefit. If she wanted to go shopping, out to eat, need money for some of her bills. She knew that my funds were limited, yet she would contact me anyway. And if I told her know she would attempt to make me feels as if I wronged her in some way.

Although we had been friends for years, I had to end that friendship. I could no longer be friends with someone whose only goal was to make withdrawals and not make deposits into our friendship. This philosophy does not only apply to friendships and other types of relationships, and it applies to our life on a whole. Sometimes we want the reward without doing the work. Many people want to be successful but are not willing to what it takes to have the abundant life that God wants you to have. Do the work and you will be rewarded for every struggle you had to endure. Invest in people, who will pour into you, help you grow, and want to be a light in your world. Those are the types of deposits you need in your relationships.

Chapter 12
The Foundation is Love, God, and Yourself

Love is the greatest gift God ever gave a man. Love is air, breathing and without it, you will cease to exist. Love gives humanity, the reason for being, and the reason for connecting with one another.

Love is synonymous with tenderness, warmth, intimacy, and an intense feeling of deep affection. Every relationship has love at the center of it; it fills itself with the good and bad, and it shapes and molds our attitudes. We sow into love by how we treat each other. The caliber of who we are is based on love. Life is all about love!

God is the center of our existence, the purpose for life, and how we are to be. He is the foundation for everything, our choices, decisions, thoughts, conduct. God gives us the passion for fulfilling His will for our lives. God's greatest achievement for all humankind is to love and create the world that honors his commandments. He sacrificed His only begotten son so that we can have a life that will bring glory to His kingdom.

I read an article in the online magazine, "Mind Body Green" that addressed fifteen choices you can do to make you happy now. I have provided five of the choices that most resonated with me:

1. **Stop "hanging out" and commit.**

Being in a committed relationship and healthy relationship makes you happier than being single.

2. **Sit down and shut up.**
   Daily meditation, super-sized satisfaction from the inside out.
3. **Take the hourly job over a salary.**
   Hourly employees are statistically happier than salaried employees.
4. **Invest in experiences rather than things.**
   This one was very real for me. I gave away all of my clothes, canceled cable, etc. I did not want material things anymore; I just wanted Jesus. To be able to release things that no longer served a purpose in my life was truly a freeing experience for me.
5. **Become a master.**
   True again, I connected myself with what I love to do, which is writing. I found my purpose and I am now a published author. T.D. Jakes said it best, "If you do not know your purpose, find something that you are passionate about; that's your purpose."

God is passion, love, air and life. Nothing is whole in our lives until we are completing one with Him.

God is the creator and ruler of the universe and source of all moral authority, the Supreme Being.

Synonyms include the following: the Lord, the Almighty, the Creator, the Maker, and the Godhead.

For God so loved the world that He gave His only begotten Son, that whoever believes in Him shall not perish, but have eternal life. (John 3:16)

Everything starts with You, God and everything ends with You. Either our habits will change as we grow or they will destroy us. Meaning, if we do something that is not worthy of good, yet continues to entertain it, and then we destroy what God has created. Choose wisely, stay grounded, never settle, and always detour negative things and people. Remember this daily as your declaration to how wonderfully beautiful you are.

PART II: WHERE ARE YOU GOING IN LIFE?

Chapter 13
History, Does that Make a Difference in a Relationship?

Does it make a difference in a relationship?
Is history what keeps the relationship going?
Is history the main reason why people stay in bad relationships?

History is defined as the study of past events, particularly in human affairs. The whole series of past events connected with someone or something.

Let's start with the basics; first, I believe history does play a role in a relationship, and that is why many people stay together. The reason for this is contentment and confront. Yes, most people who are at this level in their lives and stay in situations strictly because it feels safe and comfortable. Before you all start thinking I'm judgment, let me explain myself better and provide further clarity. I started seeing my children's father when I was nineteen years old; he was twenty. We were friends at first and developed a romantic relationship when I turned twenty-four. We got married when our daughter turned two years old. Our relationship took a turn for the worse after we wed. We fought a lot about finances. Even though we were together for four years, we were not ready for marriage; we were young and inexperienced. We felt comfortable with one another, so we felt that being married was the right thing for us to do. The longer we remained married I began to realize that God did not want this type of relationship for me. We eventually divorced after five years of marriage. Making the decision to divorce him was not easy, it was quite painful. When something is not ordained by God, it will not work.

Based on the scenario I presented, do you think I should have remained in that relationship? We had history and children together; we have known each other since I was nineteen and we were friends for four years before getting married... *Why give that up?* I gave the relationship up because it was important for me to be happy, fulfilled, maintain a peace of mind, and ultimately, joy meant more to me than anything else. My children's happiness meant everything to me, and they did not deserve to witness and experience pain at a young age, due to selfish people not wanting to change their habits and behavior. I know this is not the case for everyone, remember it is much wiser to follow God's path for your life and listen to His voice for directions. Forgive what is not right and move forward, so that the present can take its rightful place in your life. Do not be bounded by what is familiar, and you owe it to yourself to experience the happiness God created for you to have.

According to womenaccounts.com this is their take on a relationship that is wrong:

"A relationship with the wrong individual can lead to years of heartache, emotional/social damage, and even physical harm. A damaging adult partner can damage us, damage our loved ones, and even damage the way we feel about love and romance in the future. They can turn what is supposed to be a loving, supporting, and understanding relationship into the "fatal attraction." We all know to avoid people that appear insane or abusive and not select them as a dating partner. However, some individuals are better at hiding their personality and behavior abnormalities."

If you find yourself in a relationship that you are not sure if it is right for you, Pray and ask God to expose the person to you.

10 Warning Truth's to a Bad Relationship

1. **He or she is verbally abusive.**
   Many people do not see the signs of verbal abuse early in the relationship. However, verbal abuse can take several forms, such as name calling to put downs, loud rants to quiet comments, remarks that are undermining. The common denominator is the abusers need to control, to be superior, avoids taking responsibility, naming a few. It is important to note that verbal abuse can turn physical if it continues.
2. **You have been together for more than six months and had not their family or friends.**
   This should be a no-brainer. You must examine your partner a little deeper because there is truth in hiding. This person is more than likely keeping a secret from you.
3. **Your partner doesn't respect your answer when you say "no" to something.**
   If the person you are with has issues with you saying no to them, then you might have a narcissist on your hands. A narcissist is defined as individual that is vain, self-loving, self-admiring, self-absorbed, self-obsessed, and or self-centered.
4. **You do not have a sense of security in the relationship; you've broken up or had to end the relationship several times.**
   This is one I feel people tend to ignore a lot because they feel once they have had some time to be apart from one another to reflect on where things went wrong in the relationship, yet they find themselves repeating the same things. I call that being insane to do the same thing but expecting a different result.
5. **You can identify ways you have negatively influenced each other.**

Meaning, partners can negatively influence each other to do negative things, for example, if you are not a smoker or never smoked before, but your partner does, and you end up smoking to make them happy, even though, you know it is bad for your health.

6. **You cannot identify ways you've positively influenced each other.**
You have not adopted any of each other's interests or new skills. You are a great writer, and you never share your work with your partner or try to help them to enhance their abilities or develop a desire to learn a new language, such as Spanish, yet your partner has no interest in learning a new language.

7. **You are in constant contact with them. Meanwhile, they're MIA.**
If you try to contact them by calling, texting, in boxing on Facebook, and they do not respond, then you know you are not a priority, and you should give up. I honestly believe that if something is important to you, you will find the time for it. Period!

8. **Lack of trust.**
If you find that you are always wondering where your partner is, or who they are with, or assume they are doing something they shouldn't be doing, then it is time to let it go.

9. **You are in competition with one another.**
As I mentioned in my number 6 Truths, if your partner does not share your interests or value you the same things you do, then it is time to reevaluate the relationship. Now, if you and your partner are focused on developing your careers and or business and not the personal relationship between each other, then what you have is a business like a relationship.

10. Your belief/ Practices are different

This one should be at the top of your prayer request and priority list when asking God for a mate. It is vital to be connected to someone who shares the same beliefs as you. It takes more than someone going to church with you. You should share a lot of the same values, principles, and morals. The Bible warns against being unequally yoked. "Do not be yoked together with unbelievers. For what do righteousness and wickedness have in common? Or what fellowship can light have with darkness?"
(2 Corinthians 6:14 NIV)

Chapter 14
Drama: Baby Mamas

Hear me clearly ladies! I know there are a lot of great mothers out there doing right and taking care of their children. I'm one! I just want to give men a voice because there are a lot of them doing the right thing, but you rarely hear or read about it. You always hear about them being deadbeat dads.

Oh boy, in the brief story I shared about my ex, I am sure you all are thinking I am a baby mama with drama, but I am not. We'll let's explore 'Baby Mama Drama" a little more carefully, to develop solutions on how best to handle this type of situation in the scenarios presented below:

A man with four children and four different baby mamas; two of the women love him and want an exclusive relationship with him. The women do not accept or respect that he has moved and only intends to be in the life of his children.

A married man with two kids from two different baby mamas is living happily ever after with his wife and their children. One of the baby mamas makes his life miserable and interferes with the relationship he has with the child they had together. She is angry that he did not leave and is determined to make his life miserable.

A single father is raising one child because the mother is irresponsible. The mother chooses to live her life partying, fraternizing with different men, etc., instead of taking care of his kids. She does not appreciate what her child's father does and always threatens to take him to court for full custody; even though, her chances of winning are limited.

Fathers, if you have experienced any of these situations, it is important that you maintain your cool, as responding in a negative manner will lead to more negativity. Keep a positive outlook about it and never take matters into your handle. Stay strong and continue to do what is right for your children. Pray for what is not right in your situation and allow God to guide you the rest of the way.

Chapter 15
The Greatest Gift of All is Love

1 Corinthians 13:13
If I speak in the tongues of men and angels, but not love, I am a noisy gong or a clanging cymbal.
Love is patient and kind; love does not envy or boast; it is not arrogant or rude. It does not insist on its way; it is not irritable or resentful; it does not rejoice at wrongdoing but rejoices with the truth. Love bears all things, believes all things, hopes all things, and endures all things.
So now faith, hope, and love abide, these three; but the greatest of these is love.

Romans 8:28
And we know that all things work together for good to those who love God, to those who are called according to his purpose.

Romans 8:35
Who shall separate us from the love of Christ? Shall tribulation, or distress, or persecution, or famine, or peril or sword?

Hebrew was the language most used in the New Testament in the Bible. It is the language through which God communicated to His people. Love in Hebrew is "Ahava" which is made up of three basic Hebrew letters. "I give" and "love." Love is giving. Now, not only is love giving, but the process of giving develops the powerful connection between the giver and the receiver. Giving is a condition that creates and sustains love. Without giving, there is no connection that is sustaining.

Our hearts are captivated by love. We eat, sleep, and breathe love. It is who we are. *What makes the world a better place to live?* God knows our heart and the beauty that lies deep inside of us all. We connect to a good place in our world through the sharing of the stories that we tell. Our ability to laugh and produce laughter is obtained by the love we give. Love is the greatest form known to man, and our very being was created by it. God is the best representation of love. His passion for us is through the beating heart of His love. The most important lesson to learn on earth is how to love, understand why we need to love, and of if you have loved enough. Love is a priceless and the key to unlocking our true self.

Chapter 16
Are You Pregnant?

Ask yourself the following questions:
Is your womb full or empty?
How are you handling your trimesters?
Are you ready to give birth?

This chapter goes deeper into your very existence. The typical length of pregnancy is forty weeks and two hundred and eighty days. The stages of pregnancy are typically described in three-month periods known as trimesters, which are marked by distinct fetal developments. Each trimester lasts between twelve and thirteen weeks. The first trimester is when the sperm fertilizes the egg. Your baby is an embryo, the size of a grain of rice. During this period, your baby's body structure and organ systems develop. By the end of trimester one, your baby is considered a fetus. The second trimester is where your growing baby feels more real to you where you hear the heartbeat and the baby's body are growing into human form. The last trimester seems like its lasts forever, and the baby moves around a lot as it is preparing itself to be born. Women sometimes refer to the last trimester as the home stretch.

As you see for an embryo to become a full-size baby it must go through three stages of growth to enter the world. Being pregnant spiritually and not releasing or giving birth causes us to pay a greater price and the outcome lasts a lot longer. We were created for a purpose, each one of us. From the womb to earth; give meaning to your existing.

You were not created just to be roaming the world, with no desires, goals, dreams, visions, or purpose. Your mission is needed to fulfill a void in the universe; just as the developing stages of pregnancy. You have been uniquely designed for that reason.

God created gifts and talents in all of us no one was here by accident. You must discover who you are while you are here, and give birth to it so that the world can be helped by it. *Do you want to leave this great world empty?* You see, death is not the real tragedy. The real tragedy comes from not fulfilling your purpose in life and leaving the world void of your gifts. The richest place is not earth; it is the graveyard with undiscovered individuals who did not take the time to unlock the greatness that God placed inside them.

Ask yourself this last question: *What legacy will I leave behind?*

Suze Orman suggests the following eight qualities of a successful life:

1. Harmony
2. Balance
3. Courage
4. Generosity
5. Happiness
6. Wisdom
7. Cleanliness
8. Beauty

Chapter 17
Is the Wait Worth It?

Human nature tells us to go for it; why wait, it is yours, so take what you want, and you do not have to answer to anyone. That's the flesh talking, our spirit says no! The wait is worth it; you will bring glory to God's kingdom. This life we live is certainly not our own; we must do what is right, all the time. God yes! My answer is anything we do for God is worth it.

Devon and Meagan Good Franklin New York Times' bestselling authors of their newly released book titled, "The Wait: A Powerful Practice for Finding the Love of Your Life and the Life You Love." The Franklins share the story of how they met as a result of God bringing them together and their decision to abstain from having sex until they were married. God's kingdom requires a level of submission and obedience. Just like the battle of Jericho, it called for absolute obedience to God. Joshua and the Israelites conquered Jericho, and God said to Joshua, "Do not be terrified; do not be discouraged, for the Lord your God will be with you wherever you go." Joshua had faith and belief and did what God commanded. *How many of us have this type of obedience in our lives today? If God told you not to date that person because he wasn't for you, would you stop and listen to God?*

What if God said move to another state to start that business you' have been working on. *Would you step out on faith and do it?* When we wait on God for our life choices and decisions, the outcome of things becomes more meaningful and will be worth it. Think about your friendships, jobs, careers, education, homes, cars, and spouses. *Do these things add or subtract from who you are? Were they good choices and decisions, ultimately was it worth it?* Ask yourself those questions and if your answer is no, then it is time to listen to what God is telling you and make a change. God's word is worth the wait. Have the patience of Job and trust God with everything in your life. Do not make any moves without talking to God about it. My brothers and sisters in Christ, it is worth the wait.

PART III: YOUR CHOICES CHOOSES YOUR DESTINATION

Chapter 18
Moving On

God grant me the serenity to accept the things I cannot change; and wisdom to know the difference. (Romans 8:31)

"You can be pitiful, or you can be powerful, but you can be both" ~Joyce Meyer

Life at times throws up some hard situations and challenges that cause us to stress and worry about the outcome. It is important to know that the key to overcoming life's difficulties and obstacles is to move on and not to allow any situation to get the best of you. Have faith and trust in God, that you can face any situation head on, because it is in His hands. Our hindrances sometimes breed difficulties that make us feel defeated and hopeless. Here are a few examples the things that might get you feel as if you cannot move on:

- Rent
- Phone
- Car payment
- Cell phone
- Credit card

There is nothing like having bills to make you feel down when you do not have the money to pay them. My advice is that you should always take care of your roof bill; first, that is your rent or mortgage. There is nothing cute about looking good and not having a place to live. I suggest that you have the money for your essentials taken directly out of your check or bank so that you never miss a payment.

In this new technology age, Americans no longer have phones in our homes, so it is of vital importance that you pay your cell phone on time to avoid any late fees. Our phones are just as essential as our rent because it is our way of life and how we get things done.

If you have a car, it is important that you make your payments on time. Before getting a car, you should think about whether or not you need one and can you afford to maintain it. If you feel that you must have a car, consider going to a dealership that offers low APR and can provide you with a good deal. Never get a car payment that you cannot afford it will mess your credit up if you are unable to keep up with the payments. Most importantly, you do not want to pay more for a car that is not worth it.

Credit cards can serve as a helpful tool when it comes to emergencies. However, if you have the cash to pay for something, you should. Credit card companies target individuals to maximize profits off of different kinds of customers. The three most important ways credit card companies earn money are as follows: the collection of merchant fees when customers use their card, the collection of interest on balances left on the card and from the penalties of missed payments or going over credit limits. If you cannot afford to pay back what you spend with your credit cards, then you should consider not having one. Remember paying your credit card on time boosts your credit ratings, which will give you more purchasing power in the long run.

As you see all these things are a part of life, and there is not much we can do to change the structure of the system. Stop stressing, worrying, crying, or getting depressed about it. Moving on and being accountable for your finances, is the way to take control. Money can have us feeling magnificent at one point and feeling weak at another. Learn to accept and embrace the cards life has brought you to make you a stronger and wiser human being. Pray the Serenity prayer to keep your mind strong and move on to the greater side of life.

Chapter 19
Lust versus Love

"People look at the outward appearance, but the Lord looks at the heart." (1 Samuel 16:7)

Lust is defined as a very strong sexual desire for someone.

Love is defined as having an intense feeling of deep affection for a person or thing that one loves. Care very much for, feel deep affection for, hold very dear to their heart, adore, idolize, worship.

Love is the greatest gift God gave to a man.
(God's love)

For God loved the world so much that he gave his one and only Son so that everyone who believes in him will not perish but have eternal life. (John 3:16)

The Bible addresses the topic about lust in several ways:

Exodus 20:14-17 (NIT) "Do not commit adultery do not covet your neighbor's house. Do not covet your neighbor's wife, male or female, servant, ox or donkey, or anything else your neighbor owns.

Matthew 5:28 "But I say, anyone whoever looks at a woman with lust in his eye has already committed adultery with her in his heart."

Job 31: 11-12 (NIT) "for lust is a shameful sin, It is a devastating fire that destroys to hell. It would wipe out everything down."

Sex before marriage
(Porn)

Lust has its focus pleasing oneself, and it often leads to unwholesome actions and behaviors to fulfill one's desires with no regards to the consequences. Lust is about possession and greed.

As godly women and men of God, we should not entertain poke, act or succomb to lust for it will lead us down a road of destruction.

Love is a selfless act.
Love is pure
Love is God, and He showed His love by giving His only begotten son for the world, a world who still doesn't respect, acknowledge, and obey His laws and commandments. Love is everything, it is our makeup and in our genes.

This is what the Bible speaks about love:

Love is patient, love is kind, it does not envy, it does not boast, It is not proud. It is not rude; it is not self- seeking, it is not easily angered, it keeps no record of wrongs. Love does not delight in evil but rejoices with the truth. It always protects, always trusts always hopes, and always perseveres. Love never fails. (1 Corinthians 13:4-8 NIV)

Love the Lord your God with all your heart and with all your soul and with all your mind. This is the first and greatest

commandment. Love your neighbor as yourself.
(Matthew 22:37-39)

"You must love the Lord your God and obey all his requirements, decrees, regulations, and commands. (Deuteronomy 11:1 NLT)

Our goal should be to become more and more like Christ, work diligently on getting rid of our old ways and not allow sin to control our thoughts and action. We must aim to be in accordance with the scriptures which have been provided to us as a guide from God. Lust is in opposition to this idea. Nobody will ever be perfect or be without sin while still living on this earth, yet it is still a goal for which we strive for daily. An obedient life and being in good standing with God is the best way for us to live. Nothing on this earth should separate you from the Lord and His will for your life.

Pastor, Devon Franklin said this about living a life of sin:

A lot of times while I was celibate which was ten years, I became frustrated with God because I felt my good deeds were being ignored by Him. I got to a point when I said: "you know what I'm just going to live how I want to live and do what I want, no matter the consequence." Then I envisioned what that life would look like. I imagined what God would say to me when I reached the end of my life, "Devon, I had many plans for your life, however, through your acts of disobedience I can only bless you according to the level of your actions."

Live righteously, live holy, chase after God.

God has called us to live holy lives, not impure lives.
(Thessalonians 4:7)

Beloved, I am writing you no new commandment, but an old commandment that you had from the beginning. The old commandment is the word that you have heard. (John 2:7 ESV)

Chapter 20
Single Life

"The choice of wholeness while waiting for God's best."

Single is defined as only one; not one several- sole, lone, solitary, unaccompanied, alone, unmarried, unwed, unattached, and or free.

Do not give your heart to someone who can't handle it. If they do not take care of theirs, they won't take care of yours!

Real love. ~*Paul White*

A Peek at God's Perspective:

The name of the LORD is a fortified tower; the righteous run to it and are safe. (Proverbs 18:10 NIV)

God's tower not only provides safety, but it elevates us above the problem at hand, allowing us to see it from His perspective.

Single people in the Bible were Daniel, Jesus, Shadrach, Paul, Meshach, John the Baptist, Abednego, Philips four daughters, Elijah, Elisha, and Jeremiah.

Being single is not an illness; it's a part of life, and before God sends us His best, we must become our best. I'm single and strongly desire marriage, but I have realized that it is not about my timing of when a man will come along; it is God. It is time for me to fulfill my dreams, goals, purpose and building my foundation as a godly woman. I know you have heard this before, or someone has said Jesus loves you, so you are never alone. The truth is we often get that lonely feeling, needing and wanting someone during the holidays, especially Valentine's Day. I totally understand, it is a natural feeling and is only for a season. Be patient and before you know it, God's best will show up.

Here are some tips on how to stay happy living the single life by Love Coach Nicole:

1. Most important thing to do is relax. Your "singledom" will not last a lifetime.
2. Stay clean. Forget about coming home or staying home plastered. Why not take this time alone to get the help and support you need to beat your addictions once and for all.
3. Give yourself a chance. Being happy alone does not happen overnight especially if you are a recovering codependent. There will be times that you feel you are wasting your life, your life is passing you by. Best thing to do- take go for a walk or even better on a date.
4. Study something new. Figure out what you are passionate about and go for it. There is no one to hold you back but yourself. There are a few quotes chose one to speak over yourself daily

Single

I'm not single.
I'm not taken.
I'm simply on reserve.
For the one who deserves my heart.

Single
Doesn't mean
You do not know
Anything about love, it just means you
Know enough to wait for what you deserve

Appreciate being
Single Because That's
When you grow the most and with that Growth,
You come to know what you are Looking for.
Being single
Is just a status not, a destiny
Being Single Doesn't mean That you know
Nothing About Love,
Sometimes, Being Solo
Is Wiser Than Being In A wrong Relationship.

My Thoughts

God gives us the best example of holiness, clean living, integrity, order, and being a complete person. Allow Him to be your number one in your single journey, study His ways, and pray for a man like God; one who is after God's heart, His ways, and a lifestyle that represents that. Become a whole godly woman. Be around what you desire in your life. Most of all pray when you have difficulty accepting that you are single. Stay focused on the ending for the prize is you!

Chapter 21
Married Life

Marriage is defined as a legally or formally recognized union of a man and a woman (or in some jurisdictions, two people of the same sex) as partners in a relationship. Marriage is a union, alliance, fusion, mixture, mix, blend, amalgamation, combination, and or merger.

My definition of marriage is a holy commitment between men and woman witnessed by family and friends and recognized by God! A holy bond no man can break.

Then the Lord God made a woman from the rib he and taken out of the man, and he brought her to the man. The man said, "This is now bone of my bones and flesh of my flesh; she shall be called "woman" for she was taken out of a man." For this reason, a man will leave his father and mother and be united to his wife, and they will become one flesh.
(Genesis 2:22-24 NIV)

"Happy wife, happy life." ~Anonymous

He who finds a wife finds what is good and receives favor from the Lord. (Proverbs 18:22)

My five rules for a happy marriage:

1. Keep God first
2. Love unconditional

3. Forgive quickly
4. Keep your vows
5. Communicate everything

Ever since thirteen years of age, I told myself that I would only get married once because I never understood people who had two or three husband and or wives. As I got older the desire for marriage and living holy became stronger, so after getting baptized in 2004, I asked my long-time boyfriend of four years and father of our child to marry me. I know you all are saying that women should not ask men to marry them; that's backward, but so is living wrong. I wanted to please God and not my flesh. He said yes; six months later we were married. I sought God on the type of man I should marry and to know when it is the right person.

My marriage was not from God; therefore, we encountered a lot of problems. My ex-husband unfaithful, dishonest, and was not good with finances, which ultimately caused us to get evicted from our apartment. My ex-husband stole money from me and felt as if it was not a big deal since we were married. Being married did not give him the right to steal. I recall a time we were in Walmart to buy the children supplies for school, and when I got to the register, I did not have the money I thought I had, because he took. We looked like fools because of his poor financial decisions. Things got progressively worse as he began to drink alcohol heavy to point where he would pass out. It was normal for him to drink a six-pack of beer or E & J brandy on a daily basis. Things eventually led to him being verbally abusive and disrespectful in front of our children. It was hell living with him. Honestly, as I reflect upon that time, I am not sure what changed in him or why he began to act that way, but I do know that I did everything in my power to support him as his wife. After a year of dealing with this, I reached out to the family for help and guidance. He was in denial about everything; therefore, I could not help him. My life was heading down a dangerous road, fast. I was depressed, sad, lonely, and even suicidal. It got to the point that began to plan how I was going to end my life. The voices in my head were telling me daily how much I needed to end my life. I'm not worthy nobody loves me. The truth has I almost believed it. But when I thought about my children and how much they would miss me I realized that I needed to make a change.

We moved into a homeless shelter because things were not getting better at home. I wanted to be married, which is what I thought was the correct thing to do, but I did not pray for wisdom or discernment. My relationship with God was not as strong as it is today. After five years of going through complete hell and misery, I ended our marriage. My children and I deserved better, and it was my duty to make sure they lived in a household of love and peace.

Today I'm a single, godly, happy mommy, and woman. It was the best choice I could ever make. Now I'm not happy about not being married, but I'm grateful it is not to him. I will remarry again it is still my heart's desire, and God knows it. Only this time I'm allowing Him to send the best man for me.

Chapter 22
Obtaining and Maintaining

Maintain is defined as cause or enable (condition or state of affairs to continue.

Preserve, conserve, keep, retain
Provide with necessities for life or existence
Keep the same – keep steady, keep up, or keep going

Exodus 34:7
Maintaining love to thousands, and forgiving wickedness, rebellion and sin. Yet he does not leave the guilty unpunished; he punishes the children and their children for the sin of the parents to the third and fourth generation.

Obtain is defined as to come into possession of; get, acquire, or procure, as through an effort or by a request.

Always obtain things honestly; never use crooked means
Obtain the things of God that money can't buy. Not earthly possessions.

Ephesians 1:11
2 Timothy 2:10
Philippians 3:12
Philippians 3:12

Even though I have not obtained all of this or reached my goal, I continue to press on so that I can take experience all of what Jesus Christ has in store for me.

James 1:5-8
Seek God's favor in the eyes of the Lord.

"Kingdom Living"
"Divine favor from God."

Proverbs 8:35
For he who finds me, finds life and obtains favor from the Lord.

Proverbs 12:2
A good man will obtain favor from the Lord, but He will condemn a man who devises evil.

God ways are not our ways; His timing is not like our timing. I encourage you all to obtain a healthy clean and holy lifestyle that God provided for all of us. He created the bible to provide basic instructions before leaving this earth. Study and meditate on these scriptures that I provided in this chapter for you and strive each day to obtain the beautiful things of our Lord and Savior.

Chapter 23
Celebration

"Success takes focus, dictation, hard work, sacrifice, patience, perseverance, and most important a passion for what you love to do." ~*Patrice Simmons*

Success magazine Editor-in-chief, Darren Hardy posed the following suggests that you write down your definition of success.

Success to me is being in an entirely free environment filled with self-seeking, self-improvement, no fears, limitless, consistently learning, life, accomplishments, and achievements. This chapter is dedicated to the great leaders and achievers who have made a great impact in my pursuit of greatness and inspired me to continue my purpose.

Martin Luther King, Jr.
Born: January 15, 1929- April 4, 1968

Dr. King was an American Baptist minister, activist, humanitarian, and leader in the African-American civil rights movements. He is best known for his role in the advancement of civil rights using nonviolent civil disobedience based on his Christian beliefs.

Debra L. Lee
Born: August 8, 1955

In March 1996, Lee became President, Chairman and Chief Executive Officer of BET, the parent company for Black Entertainment Television.

Karen Massey and Nate Massey (My parents)
Mom Born: February 9, 1962
Dad Born: February 28, 1952

From the hard streets of Baltimore, drugs, and self-abuse God turned it all around for my parents. They are pastors of Faith Empowerment International Ministry, under the leadership of Shawanna Hope Ministries in Warner Robins, Georgia for the last seven years. God called my parents to Georgia during a mega feast conference hosted by T.D. Jakes which led them to start their journey in ministry. As pastors, they are leading and empowering women and men all over.

Karen Bethea (My Pastor), Psalmist, Recording Artist, Apostle and Author
Born: May 3, 1959

My loving Pastor Bethea got saved at the tender age of fifteen years old. She always felt different and knew God had a calling on her life. She began preaching at the age of seventeen. Her greatest challenge came in April 1997 when God called her to the pastorate. After three years of preparation, the church opened on April 9, 2000. "Set the Captives Free Outreach Center," which has grown to over 2,000 members and is a center for healing and an incubator to discover and birth destinies. This great woman has helped me to grow in areas that were needed the most. She continues to be a godly example for me and other's worldwide.

Tiffany Bethea, Mother, Author, Speaker, Mompreneur, En-

trepreneur
Born: April 22, 1983

She graduated from Hampton University obtaining a marketing degree. She wrote her first book "I Decide to Live" which birthed a women's group called the Live Circle. She continues to be a pioneer for women globally through her many businesses and women's conferences. She is an ordained minister and leads a great path for godly women. Her selfless acts are the reason this woman is a true champion and leader to me.

Aaron and Chanelle Burt

Aaron and Chanelle Burt began their journey together when they joined ACN, an MLK business where they help people save money on their bills and help you become financial feel through the joining of the company. Their mission in goal in life is to see people become who God created them to be. They pour into their businesses and impact the lives of millions of individuals. Meeting one another in the firm, Chanelle was mentored by Aaron, who is now her husband. They continue to fulfill they purpose and work together as a power couple.

Katie Marie Flicking, Co-Owner of Hello Darling a fashion clothing store.
Born: February 15, 1982

She is a Family Investment Specialist in the state of Maryland. Along with being the proud owner of Over Accessorize a nonprofit organization started in 2012. I have known this great woman since high school. She has always been a class act. She is very humble, bubbly, fun, understanding, kind, and a drive that is undeniable. I'm so proud of this visionary, focused, determined, women of God; she is certainly a pioneer in her field.

Shonnette Boone and Tichelle Squire, Founders of Divine Treasures of God (DTG)

DTG is a spiritual sorority founded in Maryland by in July 2012. I am a part of this sorority. Brokenness led me to them. Their vision was to create a sorority group, inspired by God. I was in great need to be around women who loved God, walked with integrity, and had a passion for serving. These women are that. It is five of us together. We have monthly meetings, prayer sessions, and serve the community and show. We continue to provide support for one another.

Javon Frasier
Born: July 23, 1986

The Heavenly Jewels Alliance was founded by Javon Frazier, after the completion of her first book, The Hidden Jewel. A savior of sexual abuse, Javon shares her message to help other survivors find the strength and courage to overcome their abuse and live a full, and prosperous lives.

Frances Cuesta, CEO, and Founder, Reinvent U-boot Camp CEO& founder.
Born: November 20

She is all about encouragement, empowerment, and equipping women to being whole and complete through wellness. Her vision is to provide a fitness network for women with quality services, at an affordable price. She is dedicated to helping women learn how to stay fit and healthy.

Mothyna James-Brightful, Co-Founder and Visionary Director of Heal a Woman to Heal a Nation, Inc. (HWHN) and Mothyna Hames- Brightful has a mission to work with woman and girls to build the quality of their lives and their families and community.

Monokia Nance, Co- Founder and Executive Director

With a passion for the youth and spending, almost a decade of experience in youth development reaches young people all ages and their families. Realizing that many of those families consist of single mothers it took her on a journey to focus on women. As a result, she Co-founded Heal a Woman to Heal a Nation, Inc.

Dr. Maria James, Ph.D., Co-Founder and Director of Finance

IN 2004, Maria volunteered for the first Heal a women conference, embracing the mission and vision of HWHN, Maria joined the team, serving as the director of finance of HWHN. She earned a Bachelor's degree in Biology and Public Health from Johns Hopkins University and then obtained a Ph.D. in Cellular and Molecular Medicine in 2012.

Adia Jones, Executive Manager

Adia is a dedicated mother, friend, community leader and serves as executive manager for HWHN, Adia graduated from the University of Baltimore, human services Administrative, M.S program in December 2013.

HWHN is a community-based organization I came to know this great organization when I went to their conference on

April 11, 2014; it was a life-changing the experience for me. Renewed my mind and helped further birth my purpose.

Oprah Winfrey, Former Host of The Oprah Winfrey show, CEO of Harpo Productions, Chairwoman, CEO of the Oprah Winfrey Network, Actress, Author
Born: January 29, 1954

Winfrey was born into poverty in rural Mississippi to a single teenage mother. She experienced considerable hardship during her childhood. Winfrey landed a job in radio while still in high school and began co-anchoring the local evening news at the age of 19. By the mid-1990s, she had reinvented her show with a focus on literature, self-improvement, and spirituality. Her pioneer skills and abilities are the key thing that drives her to create a work ethic that is undeniable. Her excellent leadership skills is a true quality that is to be looked upon in today's world.

Tyler Perry, Actor, Author, Playwright, Filmmaker, songwriter
Born: September 13, 1969

Perry wrote and produced many stage plays during the 1990s and 200s. Perry is known for both creating and performing as the Madea character, a tough elderly woman. Perry produces films, some produced as live recordings of stages plays. Perry has created several television shows, Tyler Perry's House of Payne, The Haves and the Have Not's. Additionally, he struck an exclusive multi- year partnership deal with Oprah Winfrey and her Oprah Winfrey Network. He continues to help the up and coming actors, filmmakers, producers, and screenwriters.

Anthony and Zenovia Andrews, Co-Founders of Max Out, Inc.

Anthony and Zenovia Andrews is a power couple that happens to my business coach. The have helped me to further my purpose as an author and writer. Zenovia is a highly sought after speaker, author, business development strategist and TV/Radio personality. She and her husband Anthony are the founders of Max Out, Inc. a successful Company committed to empowering, and teaching entrepreneurs how to increase their profits and productivity rapidly.

Devon and Meagan Good Franklin, Hollywood Power Couple and Best Selling Authors of "The Wait."

Meagan Good is an award-winning actress and producer who star as the lead in the Fox series *Minority Report*. Some of her top biggest blockbusters, including Think like a Man, *Think Like a Man Too, Anchorman 2, The Legend Continues, Stomp the Yard*, and my favorite *Eve's Bayou*. Meagan is also the co-founder of the Greater Good Foundation, nonprofit organization that advocates for the empowerment and enrichment of young women.

Devon Franklin is a Pastor, man of God who delivers God's message to people all over the world. The bestselling author of *Produced by Faith: Enjoy Real Success without Losing Your True Self*. President and CEO of Franklin Entertainment and a motivational speaker most recently produced the Sony Pictures film "Miracles from Heaven" starring Jennifer Garner. He's a graduate of the University of Southern California.

Meagan and Devon married in the summer of 2012, they reside in Los Angeles, California.

Patrice Cunningham Washington, Best Selling Author, Speaker, Coach, and Blogger

Best Selling Author of "Real Money Answers for Every Woman," Patrice Cunningham Washington is known internationally as the Wisdom & Wealth Money Maven; Patrice C. Washington is the Founder and CEO of Seek Wisdom Find Wealth, a personal finance training and development company created to move individuals from debt management to money mastery with a unique focus on helping them earn more money through discovering their purpose. Based in Atlanta, GA, Seek Wisdom Find Wealth is devoted to teaching others how to consistently eliminate financial stress and implement financial strategies that support the lifestyle they desire and deserve.

She is the author of *Real Money Answers*, a series of sensible, straightforward, question and answer style, personal finance books written to address the most common financial issues of targeted groups of individuals.

Delisha Sylvester, Founder, and CEO of Women's Elevation Magazine

Women's Elevation Magazine was created to inspire women entrepreneurs to create, share, and advise others on how to accomplish their dreams. Naturally I is a new campaign presented by Women's Elevation Magazine. They look to bring the beauty of women all around the world to the forefront.

Sarita Shares, Certified Life Coach Speaker

Sarita Shares, LLC empowers the dreamer in you to create &

develop purposeful brands, business& lifestyles.

Erica Gordon, CEO/Founder, International Bestselling Author at Moms with Dreams University

Moms with Dreams University is an online center for emerging mompreneurs who aspire to achieve their dreams without feeling guilty.

Additional Influencers:

Rosanne Reid Author, Speaker, Lifestyle Coach, Business Consultant
Halle Berry Actress, First African American to win an Oscar
Denzel Washington- Actor, Golden Globe, Tony Award
Will Smith- Actor, Nominated for two Oscars
Trent Shelton- Author, Motivational Speaker
Joyce Meyer, Joyce Meyer Ministries Best Selling Author, Evangelist, Speaker
Rick Warren, Pastor, Best Selling Author of Purpose Driven Life
Natima Sheree, Entrepreneur/ C-Suite/ TV host/Magenta

These great women and men in this chapter are true inspirations and examples of living their purpose, helping their communities and serving others.

Chapter 24
Leadership

"The very essence of leadership is that you have to have vision. You can't blow an uncertain trumpet."

The leader is defined as the person who leads or commands a group, organization, or country.

A Leader by its meaning is one who goes first and leads by example so that others are motivated, inspired, encouraged to follow them.

To be a leader, a person must have a deep- roasted commitment drive to the goal that he will strive to achieve it even if nobody follows him.

Joshua was such a man; he was publicly appointed to succeed Moses. (Numbers 27:12-23

Joshua summoned all Israel to gather at Shechem and challenged them to serve the Lord, putting before them his commitments.

"The leader has to be practical and a realist; yet must talk the language of the visionary and the idealist." ~*Eric Hoffer*

Achievable- Realistic, measurable, quantifiable, inspiring, challenging, and rooted in faith.

Attributes of Effective Leadership:

1. Persuasion skills
2. Leadership styles and personal attributes the leader
3. God is our ultimate leader.

God is with us; he is our leader. His priests with trumpets will sound the battle cry against you. People of Israel, do not fight against the Lord, the God of your ancestors, for you will not succeed. (2 Chronicles 13:12)

Meditate on these scriptures for leadership skills:

Philippians 2:3
Luke 6:31
Matthew 20:26
John 3:30
Proverbs 16:12
Psalms 78: 72
Hebrews 13:17

Notable Leaders that have made a global impact:

1. *John C. Maxwell*, World Leader
2. *Joyce Meyer*, Evangelist
3. *Napoleon Hill*, Author
4. *Darren Hardy*, Publisher of Success Magazine

Become the best you, study the great leaders before you take in their ways of being a leader then strive to be a true example of a great ambassador for the kingdom of God.

Chapter 25
You Chose

Health is defined as the state of being free from illness or injury.

Toxic means, simply put "poisonous" virulent, noxious, deadly, dangerous, and harmful chemicals.

Chemicals are defined as being a compound or substance that has been purified or prepared, especially artificially.

Fast food consists of items prepared for consumer taste buds. The ugly truth about our health is it all starts with how we view food and what we eat. For me being healthy was not always a priority. I was a girl who did not like to eat food but was big on eating sweets, cakes, pies, and cookies. I remember gaining ten pounds just from eating ice-cream. Yes, it was that bad! Truthfully, that did not cause a turning point for me to change my ways. The turning point for me was when I read scripture in the bible, "*Do you not know that your bodies are temples of the Holy Spirit, who is in you, whom you have received from God?* You are not your own. (1 Corinthians 6:19) That broke me down. Now realizing my body belongs to God, and I'm reasonable for treating it right. I cut out the ice cream cookies, cakes, and pies. I worked out twice a week, doing Zumba and turned my poor eating habits into a positive lifestyle change. It is all about your choices. You chose how you will treat your body good or bad but, whichever way you go, know it all starts and ends with you! This chapter is a guide for you to begin a healthy lifestyle because no matter how successful you are or what you achieve,

if you are not treating the body well, it is not going to matter in the end. Take comfort in knowing God will help you with your food struggles and guide you on a better path of eating and living.

Chapter 26
The Cover-Up

I remember praying to God for the ideal man to come into my life. The characteristics and attributes of the man that I desire are as follows: tall, handsome, godly, homeowner, businessman, etc. Unfortunately, the men that I have dated were the opposite of what I desired. I initially thought that I might be attracting men who are like me. I decided to change my mindset so that the right man could come along. As soon as I changed my mindset, the man of my dreams showed up. He was a minister, a man of God, an engineer, had his car and house, and well respected in his community. I knew that God sent him. Regrettably, what I thought was my dream man turned into my nightmare.

We connected through Facebook and hit it off well. We were friends at first and spent hours talking on the phone, talking about our prior relationships and the things we went through. We were both married, experienced similar issues in our marriages, and we both have four children. It almost seemed like we were a match made in heaven. Our divorces were both less than two years old and did not want to rush into anything serious right away; we wanted to see how things would go first.

We went on our first date on November 26. He came to pick me up thirty minutes early, which demonstrated that he was a punctual person. We went to a seafood restaurant in National Harbor, Maryland, which is a beautiful place, especially around the holidays. During the date, he was such a gentleman and opened doors for me, made sure I was okay with everything and offered to purchase a picture frame from this gift shop. He took me back home around 8:00 pm. Yes, it was an early date. He was just the perfect guy. You probably are thinking that he was the perfect man until his true colors showed up. Well, shortly after he dropped me off, he called me around 11:00 pm to ask me how I thought the date went. We did not even make it to our second date, yet. I told him that I had a very good time etc. Then he says something that honestly changed everything for me with him. He asked me if he could come over and spend the night with me. He wanted to have sex. Yes, he asked me for sex on our first date! Remember, he is a minister, which is totally out of order. I could not believe him. I told him no, but that we could go on another date soon. I know I should have stopped dealing with him right away, but I did not because my heart wanted him to be right, even though my gut told me what I already knew; he was not the one. Needless to say, we never went on a second date because he came up with millions of excuses of why we could not go out again. I still liked him and continued to spend time with him. I thought he was the man I prayed for. During the time we spent together, I discovered that he was controlling, selfish, mentally abusive, a liar, and had a serious porn addiction. He asked me to participate in a threesome with him. He told me that if I loved him, I would do it. This was supposed to be a man of God. I do not think so. I felt that by continuing to see him, I was helping with his morals, values, integrity.

During the time of our relationship, he played me well. I never met his children, friends, family, or anyone close to him. When I asked him about it, he told me that he was a private person. We got into an argument once, and he threatened me with his gun. I did not even know he had one. That scared me and after six months of feeling like I was his well-kept secret,

I ended things with him. I knew early in the relationship that he was not the man God sent to me, but my flesh and wants got in the way. Even though this man on paper looked right and came in the package I asked for; he turned out to be a counterfeit. Return to sender, immediately! That was a real good lesson for me to learn. If a person does not demonstrate that he is godly through his actions and not just in his words, then he is no good. I am not saying that the person has to be perfect, but must indeed possess qualities that represent God.

To my ladies out there who are thinking that if a minister behaved that way, then no one is right. That sentiment is not true. He was just not right. I am now waiting on the man God my Savior has promised me. I needed to go through that experience so that I could help other women. Never stop praying for the right man. Remember to use discernment and ask God to return to sender, if a man enters your life was not sent by him.

PART IV: A DEEPER LOOK WITHIN

Chapter 27
What If?

When we reach the age of eighteen, who we are and how we live our lives is entirely on us. Some people might feel as if they know this already, but what if I told you, that every choice, decision, challenge, behavior, thoughts, and actions were all being recorded. *Would it change the way you looked at life? What if I told you that God is recording and watching your life daily, behind a closed door?* He sees and knows the things you do not want anyone to know about. Yes, it is true He is watching us and how we chose to live our lives. How you live your life is ultimately up to you. I should let you know that being spiritually prepared for the end of life should be our top priority. *What if God had a conversation with you and told you that the way you are living is leading you down a path of destruction would you change things?* What if God showed you while you are alive what is like to be in hell.

For the wages of sin is death, but the gift of God is eternal life in Christ Jesus our Lord. (Romans 6:23 NIV)

They went down alive into the realm of the dead, with everything they owned; the earth closed over them, and they perished and were gone from the community. (Numbers 16:33 NIV)

For if God did not spare angels when they sinned, but sent them to hell, putting them in chains of darkness to be held for judgment. (Peter 2:4)

As you read through the Bible verses provided throughout this book, did you find them helpful in changing your view about how to live your life?

Some people might say that hell is not real, and don't believe that a loving God would not send anyone there. We are His children, and He does not want anyone to perish. If we do not follow the biblical instructions on how to live life, we will have to face the repercussions that come along with that!

Remember God loves us all. He does not send us to hell. We go to hell because of the way we chose to live our lives while on earth. How we live in the land determines what happens to us in the end.

Hell is a place of torment for the lost (unsaved) because everyone has sinned no one deserves to live with the holy and righteous Heavenly Father. God is a loving Father, and He offers salvation from death to all, and for those that reject the offer. God's' justice will be executed, and the wage of sin will be paid in hell.

"For the wages of sin is death, but the gift of God is eternal life in Christ Jesus our Lord." (Romans 6:23 NIV)

"So he called to him, 'Father Abraham, have pity on me and send Lazarus to dip the tip of his finger in water and cool my tongue because I am in agony in this fire." (Luke16:24 NIV)

"And the smoke of their torment will rise for ever and ever. There will be no rest day or night for those who worship the beast and its image, or for anyone who receives the mark of its name." (Revelation 14:11 NIV)

A few months ago I watched a movie called "Defending Your Life" with Meryl Streep. This film was released in 1991. The story line is about a man who was living his best life ever and then on his birthday, he got into a fatal car accident. He had the career, car, and women of his dreams. He got into a fatal car crash on his birthday. He took his eyes off of the road for a second, and when he looked up, he collided with a tractor trailer. He woke up in the afterlife, a city called, Judgment. This place was neither heaven nor hell. Judgment City is where people got judged for the life they lived while on earth. When he met the judge, a video of his life was played for him, to see if he should move forward or relive another part of his life again. Ultimately, he was not able to go ahead because of the choices when he was alive. However, Meryl Streep made a lot of wise choices and lived right, allowing her to move forward to the next chapter.

That movie was an eye opener for me. It revealed to me that our lives are indeed being recorded, daily. The choices we make are a reflection of where we will go once it is time to face the Lord. My goal and mission are to stay focused on the real prize of life (which is God), not material things that will not add any true value, continue to build the kingdom of God, forgive more, love more, have a clean mind, while renewing it daily, maintain positive thoughts versus negative ones, sinless, live righteous, and live a life pleasing to God. I will strive every day to make wise choices, turn the other check when someone does me wrong, be humble, and grateful for everything God gives me.

What is your Goal for living the life God has granted to you?
In the end, how we live, is how we will spend our eternal life. If you are not living according to God's plans, then we have to change. Live the way He wants you to live, even if you do

not believe God or hell are real or hell. *Do you think it is worth taking a chance? What if God is real can you face the true living God and have Him tell you to depart from Him because He never knew you?* Not worth it. People choose wisely, no judgments, just informing. I love you all so let's choose to serve him, obey him, trust him, and get a well done my faithful servant on Judgement day!

Chapter 28
Meditation Room

Meditation is a practice in which an individual trains the mind.

The last few chapters might have been intense and challenged you to take a look at your life, behavior, and just being a better individual. What I want you to imagine being on a beautiful, remote island where the food is great, but there are no people; it is just you. Right now, picture yourself having the life you always wanted. *Do you see it yet?* Meditate on what you desire for your life, the people you need to have in your life, the career, and everything positive you need to help you grow. *Get the picture now?*

Why meditation?

Meditation is a doorway into the unknown. It can help you to get a sense of the mystery of who we are and connect you mind with your heart.

How to meditate:

1. **Clear the mind of negative thoughts**
   This is vital to do, and it will be nearly impossible to focus yourself if your mind is filled with the things that are not going to take you to a deeper place.
2. **Posture yourself**

When your body is well- balanced, your mind will also be balanced. Imagine that your head is touching the sky.

3. **Relax and breathe**

   Paying close attention to your breathing is a great way to anchor yourself in the present moment. There is no need to regulate the breathing, just let everything be natural.

4. **Seek a quiet place**

   Whenever I meditate, I go to my prayer closet. I also call this my war room. The movie, "The War Room" inspired me to create a war room. I seek God's wisdom and guidance through prayer so that I can get myself back on track. If you are not able to get to a quiet place, go to the bathroom, or meditate at your desk office. Relax the mind goes within for a few minutes.

Meditation is an excellent way to escape from all the drama in the world. I have read stories, headlines, news that shakes me to my core; leaving me heartbroken and confused. Because of the uncertainty in this world, but once I pray, my worries and troubles are taken away by God. Through prayer, a sense of peace comes over me, and I believe that is God's way of letting me know that everything is okay. Do not allow the things of this world alter the way you view God. Keep your heart, mind, body, and soul pure.

Meditate on these Bible verses daily:

Forgiveness of Sins

John 1:9
Titus 2:14
Romans 8:1
Psalms 103: 2:4

God's love and Mercy for us

John 10:11, 15:13
John 10:10
2 Corthians 5:18-19
Psalms 103: 8-13
John 3:16

Be Well!

Chapter 29
Heaven

Heaven is a place regarded in various religions as the abode of God and the angels, a place above the sky.

When I was younger, I remember listening to a song by Stephanie Mills called "Home." I did not get the full meaning behind the song until I got older. I've provided a snippet of the song below:

When I think of home I think of a resting place a place where there's peace, quiet, and serenity. When to think of home, I think of a place where's there's love overflowing.

This almost sounds like Heaven with peace and love overflowing! The song has me thinking about God's Kingdom. She dedicated this selection to her friends that have gone to be with the Lord. The song brought joy and peace to her as she knew in her heart that they were at home with Him. Although I have not experienced Heaven, yet, I wanted to give you a feel for it. In His word, God says that you must live an obedient life and that you must walk with the Father, repent, and keep yourself holy so that you can get His will done by the end of your journey on this earth. His word that you must live an obedient life walk with the father repents keeping yourself holy so that you can get his well done at the end of your journey on earth. "He that believeth on the Son hath everlasting life: and he that believeth not the Son shall not see life, but the wrath of God abideth on him." (John3:36)

Some people might say that they do not believe that heaven is real because why would a loving God allow so many bad things happen. I once thought the same thing until I discovered that God does not permit anything to happen to us on purpose. It is our disobedience to His word and doing things our way that creates a world of destruction. If we followed his laws, principles, and lived our lives according to His commandments, only then will God heal our land.

Matthew 18:10
John 14:2
Revelation 22:1-5
John 3:16)
Philippians 3:20-21

If my people, which are called by my name, shall humble themselves, and pray, and seek my face, and turn from their wicked ways then I will hear from heaven, and I will forgive their sin and will heal their land. (2 Chronicles 7:14)

"Jesus eye's was Beautiful."

When the movie "Heaven is For Real: A Little Boy's Astounding Story of His Trip to Heaven and Back" was released in 2014, it caught my attention. I did not realize there was a book published in 2010, and I purchase it immediately and read about his journey with the Lord. His story is incredible. Colton Burpo was four years old when he got sick and had to go to the emergency room. His appendix burst. While he was in the hospital angels appeared and took him to heaven where he met Jesus. While in heaven he saw his sister that passed away before he was born, grandfather, along with seeing Mary, Paul, and King David. He described his time as mostly being spent with Jesus, and he said that Jesus' eyes were beautiful; like a ray of light! The movie is identical to the book, by the way. I took my children to see the movie. As a mother and believer, it was important for my kids to see it and they loved it. Some might people have to say this story was make-believe and that his parents put him up to it.

Now, I ask you to think about this, *how can a four-year-old boy concoct a story of meeting Jesus, his sister, Mary, and King David in heaven? What would his family gain from exposing their son to the public with such a story?* I believe he experienced this based on what the Bible says about heaven and my personal relationship with the Father. If you do not believe something like this could happen then w*hat will be the point of you serving God?*

My takeaway from the movie is that we need to do as the Father tells us. Live holy and only care about what God care's about and never doubts the experiences you encounter, just because you think that it might sound strange or unreal to other people.

(Revelation 21:21) Describes what heaven will be like. To all believers, I want you to close your eyes, open your mind from all negativity and quietly experience heaven with me. A good-looking man appears with his angels singing to you. There are twelve gates, and each one is made out of a single pearl. The street is paved with gold, and transparent glass can be seen. This is a place of peace, joy, and over pouring of love and happiness. Now open your eyes and feel His presence. Then say this to yourself daily, "I will serve the Lord all the days of my life so that I can experience the kingdom and be with the Father for all eternity."

Chapter 30
The Journey

1. **Believe in yourself**
   There is no greater love than loving who you are. You are capable of achieving great things once you discover the inner beauty that's inside of you.
2. **Stop daydreaming**
   It is time to incorporate what you have learned into your daily life. Go to the library and get books on how to be successful, develop entrepreneur skills or any book that will further your development.
3. **Prioritize your time**
   If it is not important, then do not add it to your schedule. Meaningless time spent on social media, shopping when you should be saving, and gossiping do not increase the value to your life.
4. **Pray**
   If you are a believer in Christ, like I am, start your day with prayer. Find a special place in your home for it. My special place to pray is in my closet, which I call it my war room. I have scriptures, affirmations, and quotes, where I go to daily for prayer.
5. **Exercise**
   When the body is not healthy, it can make you lazy. Take a walk, ride a bike, walk up the steps at work, and find healthy meals to eat. If you find this to be a hard task, start off slow, take it one day at a time.
6. **Breath**
   When you feel overwhelmed, relax, and live in the moment. You are the star of your show.

7. **Visualize**

   I'm a visual person, and it helps me to see the bigger picture. Especially, with me being a writer. Vision the life you desire and work off of that. It will help you to focus and stay on track.

8. **Sunshine**

   When the sun comes out it brightens up our day, it gives us a sense of hope and belief for a better day. Focus on positive things. Let go of anything negative that can hold you back.

9. **You**

   The most important person you will ever have to deal with is you. You are the creator of your choices, goals, life, and decisions. Make sure that whatever you decide to do, so that in enhances who you are and what you represent to the world.

10. **Listen**

    Any good student listens to their teacher to gain understanding about the task at hand. Listen to people who will uplift you, help you to excel you, and guide you along your journey.

Chapter 31
The Fundamentals of Life

Have you ever sat and thought to yourself what life truly is all about?

What are the essential elements I need to know about life?

Not so long ago, there was a time when I was going through my greatest trials, which caused me to open my mind to what life is all about.

The following seven fundamentals of life helped me to discover life's true meaning:

1. **Take each day, one day at a time.**
   You will have some good and bad days. Do not allow your emotions to control your outcome. Often, we stress over things that we can't change, so focus more on the things you can change about your day and stay positive.
2. **Give thanks**
   Gratitude is a key component to life. When someone does something nice for you, it teaches you to have a greater appreciation; someone holds the door for you at a store, pays for your coffee at your local coffee shop, and smiles at you. When you practice gratitude, you can take notice and reflect upon the things you are thankful for, and you will experience positive emotions, feel more alive, and have more compassion for others. A grateful heart is a

receptive heart.

3. **Be "yourself."**
You may know this already, but I would like to strongly emphasize the importance of remembering what our parents taught us about loving ourselves, no matter what! It is essential that you remain the original make-up of yourself. True authenticity comes from within; never try to duplicate what is not you.

4. **Trust your "choices."**
Why did I eat that slice of cake when I'm on a diet?
Did I say too much on this date? He is probably not going to call me again.
I totally blew that interview.
Does this sound like you? Know that the outcomes for everything we do have to do with the choices we make. Choose wisely and be confident with your decision and be at peace about it.

5. **Love more**
The greatest gift you can give the world is love. God is all about love, and it is His desire that we live in love, peace, and harmony with one another. Love is universal, and we should spread it all around to everyone.

6. **Reach for the stars**
Live every day of your life to the fullest and never take your life for granted. Believe in yourself, your dreams, and reach for the stars.

1. **Discover you**
Find out what you like to do and start doing it. Whether it is going back to school to obtain a degree or certification, become a writer, lose weight for a healthier you, and take up a hobby; no matter what, remember that you are the sparkle that shines brightly in this world.

Chapter 32
Patrice's Declaration Letter

I'm beautiful and wonderfully made in the image of God; He guides my path, keeps me from harm, and protects me with his angels. I live to serve Him, not the world. The love I have for God and my life purpose supersedes anything the world tries to give me. My journey has not always been easy and has had a lot of rocky times when my trials have gotten the best of me. But the God I serve has delivered me from them all. When I wake up in the morning, my heart is filled with gratefulness and love. I strive each day to fulfill my purpose, help people, give a smile and most importantly be a light in a world that is filled with darkness. I teach my children to live out their dreams, focus on their goals, believe in the impossible, and hope for the best in any situation that might seem hopeless. Strive to be the best you and whatever you do, keep God first.

Make your own Life Declaration. When you have a clear view and vision of what you want in your life, write a declaration to yourself and it will keep you on track for where you plan to go.

Journey to Finding You

Declaration Guide

I am_____

I believe_____

I was created to_____

_____

I hope for I love people and everything God created in this world

_____

_____

When I look at myself, I see

_____

_____

My life is all the better because

_____

I live to serve a holy God who

_____

My heart is pure and I share love

_____

I teach my children to be

_____

Chapter 33
Purpose: What Are You Created For?

If you do not know your purpose, find something that you are passionate about and you will discover your purpose. Do what you were created to do. Your purpose will impact the lives of the people you will encounter. You will make a huge difference in this world, as long you follow your purpose. Everyone has a purpose for being here on earth. Nothing happens by chance. The earth needed you and God saw fit for you to be here. It doesn't matter if you were born out of wedlock, are a single parent, a drug addicted parent, abandoned, whatever the situation, you are unique and worthy of all great things. Before I knew what my purpose was, I lived my life the way people wanted me to live. I thought everyone had to follow the same path, graduate from high school, go to college and get a degree, get married and start a family. Although many people go down this road, there is nothing wrong with doing things in that manner. It was not the path God wanted me to follow. Yes, He wants me to live an obedient life, live holy; however, He did not expect me to live by other people terms and views on how I should live my life. I discovered my purpose through finding my passion. I always loved to write poetry and essays, when I was in high school. Even when I knew my purpose, I did not walk in my purpose. Many dark storms hovered over my life and caused me to focus my attention on what was happening rather than going where God was taking me. Until one day, I broke down and wanted to end my life. Being in an abusive marriage for several years, raising children, working two jobs, and going to college, finally took its toll on me. Before attempting to take my life, I thought about my kids and how much their life would be different without me. How selfish of me to leave them, especially knowing that God had the solution to my problem.

I made a promise to God that I would walk my purpose and live for Him, follow His path for my life and live holy. That is when everything changed for me. I became a published author of a co-author project titled, "Walk in Your Purpose." Funny, how God works (laughs). I wrote articles about my life in two magazine articles. To date, I have published three books and "Journey to Finding You," will be my fourth book. When you say yes to God's will and His purpose, nothing is impossible or imaginable. Great things will happen in your life. There is no greater feeling than knowing that you are living the life God created for you while discovering who you are in the meanwhile. If you are not sure, your purpose here is a few scriptures to help guide you along your journey.

Psalm 138:8
The Lord will fulfill his purpose for me; your steadfast love, O Lord, endures forever. Do not forsake the work of your hands.

Romans 12:2
Do not be conformed to this world, but be transformed by the renewal of your mind, that by testing you may discern what is the will of God, what is good and acceptable and perfect.

Psalm 73:26
My flesh and my heart may fail, but God is the strength of my heart my portion forever.

Ephesians 1:11
In Him we have obtained an inheritance, having been predestined according to the purpose of him who works all things according to the counsel of His will.

Revelation 4:11
Worthy are You, our Lord and God, to receive glory and honor and power, for You created all things, and by Your will, they existed and were created.

Galatians 1:15
But when He who has set me apart before I was born, and who called me by His grace.

Matthew 6:33
Seek first the kingdom of God and his righteousness, and all these things will be added to you.

Jeremiah 29:11
For I know the plans I have for you, declares the Lord, plans for welfare and not for evil, to give you a future and hope. Then you will call upon Me and come and pray to Me, and I will hear you. You will seek Me and find Me when you seek Me with all your heart.

Chapter 34
Life Goals

Goal-The object of a person ambition or effort; an aim or desired result.

A goal is not a thought or idea that is not achieveable.

In life, we all have goals, dreams, ambitions that we want to make in this world. To make your vision, dream a reality, you have to put faith behind and create goals to achieve it.

"Reason! The reason is the blueprint. Make a Plan and modify it as new information comes." *~Hill Harper*

Bishop T.D Jakes said, "Reason is the blueprint for our lives." *What is your plan?* (Habakkuk2:2) He emphasized the importance of writing down your vision and plan. He believes that the essence we should all have a personal vision and plan for our lives. It is our job to discover what our purpose is and walk in that purpose. As we get new information that requires action, we modify the plan to ensure we create personal success. The journey will not be easy as we hit the peaks and valleys, but keeping the Reason before you will keep your focus. Despite all the things we are here to grow our faith. We must do as Paul said, "Brothers and sisters, I do not consider myself yet to have taken hold of it. But one thing I do: Forgetting what is behind and straining toward what is ahead, I press on toward the goal to win the prize for which God has called me heavenward in Christ Jesus." (Philippians

3:13-14 NIV) We must press toward the purpose that is designed for Us!

Follow God's path for your life, do not try to be like anyone but who God designed you to be. You will be rewarded for your efforts as you seek His will. God has given you talents and gifts, which will breed great things for you. Sometimes, I believe that people have an identity complex. They do not know who they want to be from day-to-day. Looking at other people fulfilling their dreams wishing to be like them. Not realizing you are uniquely designing from God. Embrace it, live it, breathe it, be YOU!

Believe in yourself, despite what others think about you.
Let go of your fears.
Never doubt yourself.
You are special, worthy of all great things.
Stay in your lane.
Focus your attention on what matters the most about your goal.
Determine why you want to achieve the goals you have identified and how you will achieve them.

When I started to put my efforts into my goals, the goals became a reality. I will share two of the goals I had with you. A few months back I gained thirty pounds, and my thighs were rubbing together, and my face was fat. I got tired of not being able to fit into my jeans or my other outfits. I decided that it was time to lose some weight. I knew that dieting was not going to work because they worked temporarily. I had to make this a lifestyle change.

I had to connect my mind with my heart. Realize that my body is God's temple and had to treat it well.

Tips:

- Aim to be the healthiest I could be.
- Set realistic goals.
- Plan my workouts.
- Focus on positive things.
- Connect with others who are on the same path to healthy eating.

In two months, I lost twenty of those thirty pounds. I am very proud about my progress. The journey was not easy, but it was worth it. We need to be healthy and complete if we desire to live the life God has intended for us. Give yourself permission to be happy and love the person you are. I continue to live a healthy lifestyle; mind, body, and soul.

Without a goal in mind you probably will not reach it. The harsh reality is that we do not work hard at the things we say we want. We dream about our life and then wake up and eat chips in front of the TV for hours and then wonder why our life is the way that it is.

My Advice:

- Work at the goals you want to achieve
- Be consisted of your goals
- Learn your craft, skill, daily, and stay focus!

PART V:
DEFINING YOUR PURPOSE

Chapter 35
Destination

Destination-The place to which one is going or directed. The ultimate purpose for which something is created or intended.

Archaic-An act of appointing or setting aside for a particular purpose.

My definition of destination is the ability to ask the Lord for guidance for your life and the discipline to write down your goals with the intention of achieving them. A plan is a set of actions a person has thought of as a way to do or achieve something. Through hard work and patience, you will be able to focus and leave the cup half empty, making room for it be a full.

God's definition of destination is that the heart of man plans His way, but the Lord establishes his steps. (Proverbs 16:9)

By faith Abraham, when called to go to a place he would later receive as his inheritance, obeyed and went, even though he did not know where he was going. (Hebrews 11:8) Then they were willing to take him into the boat, and immediately the boat reached the shore where they were heading. (John 6:21)

In this life, every beginning has an ending and every journey has a destination! Whether you are traveling by land, sea, or air, you are headed somewhere. Finding your purpose is life's biggest challenge; therefore, you must know where you were born. Whether you realize it or not, you are here for a reason! Even if your birth was an "accident" God has a mission for your life that no one else can fill. Some of the most miserable people in the world are those who either do not believe this or who have not yet discovered their purpose. Living without purpose leads to all manner of evils that people inflict upon themselves and others.

I read an article in Bible Bay about destinations, see below:

Today, as I seek to understand God's purpose for my life, I will…

1. Listen for His voice, respond to His desires and praise His name.
2. Use my gifts and possessions to make someone else's life a little easier.
3. Be authentic, reject mediocrity, and pursue creativity.
4. Demand more of myself than I do of others.
5. Learn something new and pass it on.
6. Challenge the status quo, question the rules and take the time to dream.
7. Take care of myself.
8. Find a tangible way to express gratitude to a family member or friend.
9. Be self-forgiving when I fail to measure up to my expectations.
10. Plan for tomorrow, but understand that "life" happens today.

You see life is not a destination it is a journey. You are not going to reach your goal until you achieve your life's purpose and victory. Our destination is determined at the end of our life. And throughout the chapters of this book, you learned that your choices and decisions will be the deciding factor about your destination. I encourage you to choose wisely in this life we live, seek God every day, and never allow your past to interfere with your purpose and destination.

Chapter 36
Difficult Roads Often Lead to Beautiful Destinations

God is eager for you to test His promise. "I will instruct you and teach you in the way which you should go; I will counsel you with My eye upon you." (Psalm 32:8)

I am sure of this that He who started a good work in you will carry it on to completion until the day of Christ Jesus (Philippians 1:6)

And now, just as you accepted Christ Jesus as your Lord, you must continue to follow Him. Let your roots grow down into Him, and let your lives be built on Him. Then your faith will grow strong in the truth you were taught, and you will overflow with thankfulness. (Colossians 2:6-7)

Commit to the Lord whatever you do, and He will establish your plan. (Proverbs 16:3)

On our journey, we must continually avoid Satan, confess our sins, and forsake them.

If we confess our sins, He is faithful and just to forgive us our sins, and to cleanse us from all unrighteousness. (John 1:9)

Rich Dubose's definition of destination is as follows:

Prescription: Create some space for reflective thought and ask God to help you understand your life purpose. Make a list of your gifts and abilities. Write down a series of short life statements that reflect your convictions and ideals. Assemble these into a statement of purpose for daily reference. Be open to change and make adjustments as God leads.

Lastly, fight the good fight of faith. Take hold of eternal life to which you were called when you made your good confession in the presence of many witnesses. (1Timothy 6:12)

Chapter 37
Walk in Your Victory

Victory – achievement of mastery or success in a struggle or endeavor against odds or difficulties.

Examples of Victory in the Bible:

Deuteronomy 20:1-4
When you go out to battle against your enemies and see horses and chariots and people more numerous than you, do not be afraid of them; for the LORD your God, who brought you up from the land of Egypt, is with you. When you are approaching the battle, the priest shall come near and speak to the people. He shall say to them, 'Hear, O Israel, you are approaching the battle against your enemies today. Do not be fainthearted. Do not be afraid, or panic, or tremble before them, for the Lord your God is the one who goes with you, to fight for you, against your enemies, to save you.

Psalm 60: 11-12, Romans 6:6-22
'O give us help against the adversary, for deliverance by man is in vain. Through God, we shall do valiantly, and it is He who will tread our adversaries.

1 Corinthians 15:57
Thanks be to God, who always lead us in triumph in Christ, and manifests through us the sweet aroma of the knowledge of Him in every place.

Tips to staying victorious:

- Never stop winning in your life
- Believe all things are possible
- Have faith
- Keep achieving
- Celebrate you
- Over the battles in your mind

My Thoughts

Victory is a state of mind that connects you with oneself. You have to believe that no matter what life brings your way, you will overcome the battle and get the victory. God is the master and achiever of victory. He survived the cross, rose again, and overcame the world. You are the master of your life and the finisher of your win.

Chapter 38
Kingdom

But seek first his kingdom and righteousness, and all these things will be given to you as well. (Matthew 6:33 NIV)

Seek the kingdom of God above all else, and live righteously, and he will give you everything you need. (Matthew 6:33 NLT)

But the saints of the Highest One will receive the kingdom and possess the kingdom forever, for all ages to come. (Daniel 7:18)

And the Lord will be king over all the earth; in that day, the Lord will be the only one, and His name the only name. (Zechariah 14:9)

What is the Kingdom of God?
By: United Church Of God

The word translated "kingdom" throughout the New Testament is the Greek word basilica, which denotes "sovereignty, royal power, and dominion. A careful examination of the Bible reveals that the next phase of the kingdom of God is nothing short of a world-ruling monarchy that God will establish on this earth through Jesus Christ.

The wonderful news of the coming kingdom of God is the heart and core of Jesus Christ's message for humanity. Jesus will return to earth and establish this kingdom. He will be the ruler of the kingdom of God. Consider this prophecy about Jesus Christ's return:

"Then the seventh angel sounded: And there were loud voices in heaven, saying, 'The kingdoms of this world have become the kingdoms of our Lord and His Christ, and He shall reign forever and ever" (Revelation 11:5)

"Then the sovereignty, power and greatness of the kingdoms under the whole heaven will be handed over to the saints, the people of the highest. His kingdom will be an everlasting kingdom, and all rulers will worship and obey him"
(Daniel 7:27 NIV)

My Thoughts

God loves you even in your darkest hours. He comforts you even in your darkest moments. He forgives you even in your most dismal failures. Understand that there are a few things in life as important as speaking God's Word every day. When you confess His promises over your life and circumstances, you are making him the center of your world. Choosing to allow Him to walk with you, talk with you, and have His way in every area of your being makes you a mature person and develops you into a true warrior for the kingdom of God. Remember any battle or hardship we face, trust God and not worry about tomorrow. Sometimes it may be difficult to understand this because we want to handle things our way. I ask you to humble yourselves, make a clear decision to use wisdom, believe in all things, and never doubt what God can do during those tough times.

God is Real, God is Priceless, and God is worth it!

Chapter 39
Keys: What Do You Desire in Life?

Do you hold the keys to unlocking your future?
What type of key do you have in your life?
Are you losing your keys, or taking a hold of them?

Let's explore the meaning of keys in relation to your life in detail:

I will give you the keys of the kingdom of heaven; whatever you bind on earth will be bound in heaven, and whatever you lose on earth will be loosed in heaven." (Matthew 16:19NIV) This scripture tells us that God will give us the keys of the kingdom to be with Him. Whatever we do on this earth for Him, will be given to us in heaven. Meaning our purpose in life is that we make choices and decisions that will connect us to Him if we want to do what is holy and righteous while on earth. Which leads me right to the three questions I posed at the beginning of this chapter. The type of keys you hold in your life is vital in your journey. *Why?* It sets the tone for who you are and where you are going with God. Fear, doubt, and uncertainty, only get in your way. When I first started out with discovering my purpose, I had to examine the things I liked to do. I hit a roadblock in that process and could not figure out what my purpose was. I thought going to college would help me, but soon after arriving I found myself uninspired, lost, and heading nowhere fast. Realizing college was not for me; nothing wrong with a higher education, I believe we all should be lifelong learners and achievers.

The direction and road each one of us takes will be different. So my quest began to finding my purpose. Only this time I asked God to help me, I asked Him, "*What did you create in me to do in this world?*" He answered, "*What are you passionate about?*" I replied that my passion were the things I loved to do, regardless of whether or not I am being paid. I started to explore. The writing was at the top of my list, along with being a life coach. I love people good, bad, ugly, nice, and mean; it doesn't matter, I love all people. My heart is driven towards people who are lonely, brokenhearted or simply going through in their life. While I found my passion, I did not know my purpose. I logged into Facebook one day and saw a quote from T. D. Jakes, "If you cannot figure out your purpose, figure out your passion. For your passion will lead you right into your purpose." That was the key that unlocked the person I was created to be. My purpose began from that point. Everything I do at this point is my purpose, and I do it with my heart, compassion, and confidence.

The types of keys you have are vital to your growth and purpose. Bitterness, lack of forgiveness, strife, and hate will hurt you in your progress. God cannot work in you if darkness lies inside of you.

Strive for peace with everyone, and for the holiness without which no one will see the Lord. See to it that no one fails to obtain the grace of God; that no "root of bitterness" springs up and cause trouble, and by it many become defiled.
(Hebrews 12:14 ESV)

But God shows his love for us in that while we were still sinners, Christ died for us. (Romans 5:8 ESV)

Be kind to one another, tenderhearted, forgive one another, as God in Christ forgave you. (Ephesians 4:32 ESV)

The only way to win and be all that God has called you to be is to have love in your heart, seek to find the best in others, forgive often, believe in the impossible, and never give up on you!

Tips:

- Keep a pure heart
- Remain whole
- Complete your vision

You must take control of your keys and do not allow people to interfere with that. The vision God gave you is for you, and it does not matter if people cannot see it. Do not continue listening to what others think or feel about you if it has nothing to do with your purpose. Do not give anyone permission to have access to your heart, which is the guiding place to where you and God connect.

"If the key to your dreams is locked up in your fears, doubts, strife, lack of forgiveness; remove them to gain hold of your life and purpose." *~Patrice Simmons*

Chapter 40
Maya Angelou

Born Marguerite Ann Johnson on April 4, 1928, was an American author and poet. Scholar, Joanne M. Braxton called "America's most visible black female autobiographer. " She is best known for her series of six autobiographical volumes, which focused on her childhood and early adult experiences. The first and most highly acclaimed, I Know Why the Caged Bird Sings (1969), depicts the first seventeen years of her life. She earned an international book award. She has been awarded over thirty honorary degrees and was nominated for a Pulitzer Prize for her 1971 volume of poetry.

As a poet and author myself, Maya Angelo work has been an inspiration for me. I remember reading some of her poetry when I was in high schools which lead me down a path of writing a lot of poems. Here are some snippets of my favorite poems she has written:

Phenomenal Woman

Pretty women wonder where my secret lies. I'm not cute or built to suit a fashion model's size, but when I start to tell them, they think I'm telling lies. I say, it is in the reach of my arms the span of my hips, the stride of my step, and the curl of my lips. I'm a woman a phenomenal woman; that's me.

Cage Bird

The free bird leaps on the back of the wind and floats downstream till the current ends and dips his wings in the orange sun rays and dares to claim the sky. But a bird that stalks down his narrow cage can seldom see through his bars of rage his wings are clipped, and his feet are tired, so he opens his throat to sing. The caged bird sings with a fearful thrill of the thing unknown, but longed for still, and his tune is heard on the distant hill, for the caged bird sings of freedom.

Still I Rise

You may write down in history with your bitter, twisted lies, you may tread me in the very dirt but still, like dust, I'll rise. *Does my sassiness upset you? Why are you beset with gloom?* 'Cause I walk like I have got oil wells Pumping in my living room. Just like moons and like suns, with the certainty of tides, just like the hopes springing high, still I'll rise. You may shoot me with your words, you may cut me with your eyes, you may kill me with your hatefulness, but still, like air, I'll rise.

Equality

You declare you see me dimly through a glass which will not shine, though I stand before you boldly, trim in rank and marking time, you do own to hear me faintly as a whisper out of range while my drums beat out the message and the rhythms never change. Equality and I will be free. Equality and I will be free. Hear the tempo so compelling, hear the blood throb in my veins. Yes, my drums are beating nightly, and the rhythms never change. Equality and I will be free. Equality and I will be free.

Chapter 41
When I Think About Myself

I almost laughed at myself, I almost laughed myself to death, and my life has been one great big joke. The dance that walks, like a song that speaks, I laugh so hard I almost choke when I think about myself. My folks can make me split my side, I laughed so hard I nearly died, the tales they tell, sounds just like lying, they grow the fruit, but eat the rind, I laugh until I start crying When I think about my folks.

Maya Angelou's poems resonated with me and have helped me a lot in my growth. As a writer and poet, her words are like fire that puts out the smoke in the earth. So much wisdom, power, and truth can be found in Maya Angelou's poems. Thank you for sharing your gift with us for the entire world to see and be a part of generations to come.

I've written a few poems that embody the true essence of who I am and what is to come for me.

Queen

A queen of many tribes flying like butterflies, holding the spanks of each waist side. Sending the depth of your kiss, that is felt inside. I cannot lie; your eyes tell me lies. A queen of many tribes, the Ashanti's, Zulu, Afar, all equates to our heritage.

Queens shine your light on the sky; raise your voices high

for all the heavens to open your beautiful smile. The peak of a women's touch, the range of your inner heart, while your flesh is at rest, let your spirit connect queen, connect to purpose dreams, and belief in oneself,
Rise, rise like a Queen…

Men

When I was young, I used to Watch behind the curtains As men walked up and down the street. Wino men, old men. One day they hold you in the Palms of their hands, gentle, as if you Were the last raw egg in the world. Then they tighten up. Just a little. The first squeeze is nice. A quick hug. Soft into your defenselessness. A little More. The hurt begins. Wrench out a Smile that slides around the fear. When the Air disappears. Then the window draws full upon your mind. There, just beyond the sway of curtains, men walk. Knowing something. Going someplace. But this time, I will simply stand and watch.

Angel

To believe is to see angels dancing among the clouds, sing His praise all around.
Knowing we are not alone, our life is a gift, and this is the time to cherish it.
Using our gifts to connect with people all around, believing in the impossible knowing angels are surrounding, us all.

Relationships

The building block of life
The stepping stone to all humankind
Nothing exists without it, greed, hate, fear, and doubt has

corrupted it, with love in my heart; peace in my soul, knowing God is love, everything I do will follow it, being still in dark places, shine brightly in light, my time will come to fall in the right one's hands.

Vision

Father grace us with Your Vision so that purpose can ignite us.
While Your love guides us, let Your peace consume us.
Healing waters reign over our lives.
Giving no authority to the enemy, the breath of life refreshes our mind.
Breaking the chains of bondage and despair from our lives.
Seeking your love, not the love of humankind.
Let no attacks become our pain.
As we go behind the veil for your refugee to gain purpose and knowledge to birth out Your Vision
Let us all run with our Visions.

www.ingramcontent.com/pod-product-compliance
Lightning Source LLC
Chambersburg PA
CBHW031631160426
43196CB00006B/371